Latin American
cookbook

Opposite: Stuffed Crabs *(Casquinhos de Caranguejo)*, recipe on page 39.
Previous page: Bahian Soup *(Sopa Bahiano)*, recipe on page 25.

Latin American cookbook

Lynelle Tume

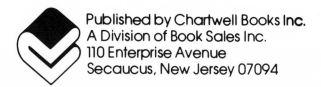

Published by Chartwell Books Inc.
A Division of Book Sales Inc.
110 Enterprise Avenue
Secaucus, New Jersey 07094

Photographs: Wayne Murphy
Illustrations: Jayne Sanderson

This edition
Published by Chartwell Books Inc.
A Division of Book Sales Inc.
110 Enterprise Avenue
Secaucus, New Jersey 07094

First published by Paul Hamlyn Pty Limited
176 South Creek Road, Dee Why West, Australia 2099
First published 1979
© Copyright Paul Hamlyn Pty Limited 1979
Produced in Australia by the Publisher
Photographs: Wayne Murphy
Cover photograph: Reg Morrison
Illustrations: Jayne Sanderson
Typeset in Australia by G.T. Setters Pty Limited
Printed in Hong Kong

ISBN: 0-89009-277-X

Acknowledgements

I owe a special debt of gratitude to many people in markets, bakeries, restaurants and hotels in Brazil, Argentina, Peru and Chile, who shared their cookery knowledge with me and thus helped make my task easier.

I should also like to thank my good friends from Argentina Dr Adalberto Vieyra, his parents Dr Manuel and Celia Vieyra and Mary Vieyra for their hospitality. Celia and Mary helped me in their kitchen, and very kindly passed on to me many family recipes.

Dr Angel Lopez and his father gave invaluable advice on Argentine food traditions.

I am also indebted to the illustrator of this book, Jayne Sanderson, who lived near me in Rio with her family and who also travelled through Latin America. Her illustrations admirably capture the spirit and flavour of the country.

Finally, my thanks to Dr Leopoldo de Meis, who made it possible for my family and I to live in Brazil.

Lynelle Tume

Contents

The Food of Latin America

Latin American cooking is as varied and exciting as the continent itself. Over the course of centuries Indians, Europeans and Africans have all helped make the country's cuisine the unique blend of traditions that it is today.

The Portuguese settlers (in Brazil) and the Spanish (in the rest of Latin America) brought with them the many European customs and recipes that survive today, though often in altered forms.

Many years before any Europeans arrived on their shores, the Indians throughout the country had developed a sophisticated style of cooking and varied ways of using local foods.

The Indians experimented with herbs and spices and introduced European explorers to the tomato, which was unknown in Europe at the time. In turn, the Europeans introduced onions, garlic and dairy produce into the Indians' diet. Traditions associated with these foods are still respected today.

In their turn, the Portuguese in Brazil and the Spanish throughout the rest of Latin America brought with them the many European customs and recipes that survive over the country today. In later years German beer, Italian pasta and French cooking techniques were also introduced. It was at this time that experiments were conducted with vineyards, and the Latin American wine industry began to develop.

When the Portuguese brought slaves from Africa to Brazil, a new note was added to the cuisine of that country. The Africans brought palm trees, giving palm oil or *dende* which is now a feature of Brazilian cooking. Coconuts also became an important culinary feature. Many African recipes originated from the custom of serving offerings to the gods, necessitating precise and traditional preparation and serving of foods; in fact in many parts of Brazil today, clay bowls and pots can be seen containing strange food offerings. These ritual preparations form part of the African-based 'black magic' religions.

The geography of Latin America has had a profound effect on its cuisine. Meats, tropical fruits, vegetables, grains and seafood are all specialities of the different countries, according to their climates. In fact, the cooking styles of many Latin American countries tend to overlap, particularly where climates are similar and therefore where similar foods are grown.

Mexico, the most northerly country in Latin America, has large arid areas and equally large mountainous regions, and has had to cope

11

with many problems in producing foods. However, the cooking of the country's original inhabitants, the Aztec Indians, has survived very strongly — indeed, Indian cooking methods are more widespread in Mexico than in any other Latin American country. Favourite Mexican foods are corn, beans, rice and chillies. Corn is used in many forms, from fresh corn on the cob to the cornmeal flour *(masa harina)* which is used to make staple foods such as *tortillas* and *tamales*. This cornmeal flour is made from white corn, which is first dried and soaked in lime water to remove the kernel skins and then ground to a paste. The paste is dehydrated to make the *masa harina*. There is no substitute for it, because it is made from white corn — not yellow — and therefore its effect is very different from cornflour (cornstarch) or cornmeal.

Instant *masa* dough is available in the United States, but in Australia it is impossible to buy cornmeal flour or *masa harina* in any form. I have tried using cornflour and cornmeal substitutes made from yellow corn, but the resulting flavour and texture have been poor. However, some recipes are included for

those who can obtain *masa* dough.

Tortillas are the basis for many Mexican dishes. These flat pancakes are made from corn flour and appear in a variety of forms, either soft or crunchy. Sometimes they are used as a plate, a spoon or a scoop. Usually they are stuffed with a filling and rolled up. There are many kinds of tortillas, including *tacos*, *tostados*, *enchiladas*, *tamales* and *quesadillas*. I have provided recipes for several varieties.

Frozen ready-made *tortillas* can be bought in the United States, and in areas with large Mexican populations there are *tortillerias* where they may be purchased freshly-made. Australia is not so fortunate, but some specialist food shops do stock frozen *tortillas*.

Beans and soups are also integral features of Mexican cooking. Beans are the staple of the Mexican diet, and are served at virtually every meal in one form or another. The thick stew-like soups characteristic of many Latin American countries are an important part of Mexican cuisine.

Chillies are so closely associated with Mexican cooking that it is difficult to imagine

12

any Mexican food without them. I have given several recipes that use a generous proportion of these hot, spicy peppers; if you feel that there is too much chilli in some of them, reduce the quantity. The recipes are very tasty even without the hotness and sweetness that chillies give.

On the other side of the Panama Canal, Venezuela and Colombia grow a wide range of foods. The high, cold areas grow excellent potatoes, while exotic fruits such as avocados and coconuts are found in the tropical lowlands.

Most of the meat in this area is tough, for the animals are mountain-reared, but the cooking methods more than compensate for this. Meat stews and ragouts feature in much Venezuelan and Colombian cooking. There is also an excellent and varied supply of seafood from the coastal regions. Both countries grow some of the world's best coffee, for the mountain, shade-grown coffee plants produce a far superior coffee to that found in the neighbouring country of Brazil.

Brazilian food is so varied that it is difficult to classify as any one style. In the north the predominance is African, a heritage of the negroes brought as slaves to the sugar plantations. This cooking is exciting, spicy and colourful and the sweets which use masses of sugar, coconut and eggs are rich and delicious. The further south one travels the more European the food, because the south of Brazil has large communities of Germans and Italians. As in Mexico, beans are part of the daily diet, and black beans are an essential ingredient in *feijoada completa*, the great national dish which combines them with smoked and cured meats and is garnished with fresh fruit. Vegetables are prepared with great flair and imagination, offering piquant contrast to some of the more solid soups, stews and meat dishes characteristic of the cuisine. In Brazil rice is the main accompaniment to meals, rather than potatoes; more rice is consumed in Brazil than in many Asian countries. It is difficult to imagine a truly Brazilian meal without *farina*, the white manioc meal that is sprinkled on many foods.

Large parts of Argentina, Bolivia, Chile, Ecuador and Peru once belonged to the mighty empire of the Inca Indians and the cuisine of

13

these countries still has a strong Indian influence. Peru and Chile on the west coast have food-producing problems because of the Andes, the high mountain range which forms the backbone of Peru and which stretches through part of Chile. The narrow coastal plain of Peru, with the Andes on one side and the Pacific Ocean on the other, is extremely dry and barren, and the very low rainfall in Peru and Chile makes the cultivation of crops very difficult.

Consequently one would not expect grains and cereals to form a large part of the Chilean and Peruvian cuisine. However, in Peru the potato was developed. In the Andes grow an incredibly large number of potato varieties, some of which are unknown to the rest of the world. The Peruvians even freeze-dry their huge potato crop to ensure that supplies are available later. The potatoes are frozen on the ground during the evenings when the temperature is below zero, and are thawed there during the day as the sun warms the air. They freeze again at night, and this process continues until they are dehydrated — though they are crushed and trampled as well. At the end of

this process, the potato is dry and cardboard-like; it is then stored. Corn is grown in some parts of Peru, where it accompanies the potato at almost every meal.

An icy, plankton-rich current flows up from the south and washes the Peruvian shores, so that the seafood of this country is varied and delicious. Much of it is served with piquant and exotic sauces and side dishes.

The same current that supplies the Peruvian coast washes over the Chilean shores. Some Chilean soups *(chupe)* and their seafood stews *(caldilo)* are unforgettably delicious. Even the ingredients are unusual; as well as fish, scallops and prawns, Chileans use generous quantities of conger eel *(congrio)* and abalone *(locos)* which are delicious in their brothy stews. As elsewhere in Latin America, the *corvina* or sea bass, a large white-fleshed fish, is used extensively, and the pink and white shellfish called *conchita* is very popular.

Argentines tend to consume a larger proportion of beef to vegetables than do other Latin Americans. To accompany meat dishes, from the simplest baked meats to the colourful and elaborate *matambres* and stews, a side dish of

puréed corn, onions, garlic, peppers, cheese and spices known as *humitas* (page 54) is served. Sometimes this is wrapped in corn husks and steamed, and is then called *humitas en chala*.

In Argentina, as in Chile, the *empanada* comes into its own. These tiny meat pies, spicy and delightful, are eaten at all hours of the day. The pastry encloses a tasty meat-based filling, the ingredients of which vary according to the region in which it is prepared. The locals know immediately what extra ingredients will be included — whether potatoes, olives, eggs or chillies. *Empanadas* can be fried *(fritos)* or baked *(al horno)* so that they can be enjoyed in many ways. I have given several *empanada* recipes in this book.

The sweets of Chile and the Argentine are excellent, as are those in all Latin American countries, but the pastries with fruit or caramel fillings are particularly delicious.

Bolivian cuisine is similar to that of its neighbours Argentina, Brazil, Peru and Chile, with many dishes being Spanish in origin. The cuisine of Paraguay and Uruguay is similar to that of Bolivia, though there is a strong Italian influence in Paraguay.

This book is not intended to provide a total coverage of Latin American cookery, since some typical dishes specify ingredients that are difficult to obtain elsewhere and for which there is no adequate substitute. I have selected the most typical Latin American dishes and adapted them, since many of the tropical fruits and vegetables that form an integral part of Latin American cookery are widely available. I believe this is preferable to producing a comprehensive cookbook that uses many unprocurable ingredients, since this is most frustrating and destroys much of the enjoyment of experimenting with a new cuisine.

My suggestions for serving methods and accompaniments to meals are not necessarily traditional, since they include more vegetable and salad dishes than most Latin Americans use. They are intended merely as ideas, because choice of fruit and vegetables so often depends on personal preference, seasonal availability and freshness.

I hope that the colour and flair of Latin American cooking will appeal to you and that you will find a place for it in your kitchen.

15

Weights and Measures

The metric weights and metric fluid measures used in this book are those of the *Standards Association of Australia*. A good set of scales, a graduated Australian Standard measuring cup and a set of Australian measuring spoons will be very helpful and can be obtained from leading hardware and kitchenware stores.

All cup and spoon measurements are level:
- The *Australian Standard measuring cup* has a capacity of 250 millilitres (250 ml).
- The *Australian Standard tablespoon* has a capacity of 20 millilitres (20 ml).
- The *Australian Standard teaspoon* has a capacity of 5 millilitres (5 ml).

In all recipes, imperial equivalents of metric measures are shown in parentheses, e.g. 500 g (1 lb) beef. Although the metric yields of cup and weighed measures are approximately 10 per cent greater than the imperial yields, the proportions remain the same. Therefore, for successful cooking use either metric or imperial weights and measures — do not mix the two.

New Zealand, British, United States and Canadian weights and measures are the same as Australian weights and measures except that:

(a) the Australian and British Standard tablespoons have a capacity of 20 millilitres (20 ml) whereas the New Zealand, United States and Canadian Standard tablespoons have a capacity of 15 millilitres (15 ml), therefore all tablespoon measures should be taken generously in those countries;
(b) the imperial pint (Australia, New Zealand and Britain) has a capacity of 20 fl oz whereas the US pint used in the United States and Canada has a capacity of 16 fl oz.

The following charts of conversion equivalents will be useful:

16

Imperial Weight	Metric Weight
½ oz	15 g
1 oz	30 g
2 oz	60 g
3 oz	90 g
4 oz (¼ lb)	125 g
6 oz	185 g
8 oz (½ lb)	250 g
12 oz (¾ lb)	375 g
16 oz (1 lb)	500 g
24 oz (1½ lb)	750 g
32 oz (2 lb)	1000 g (1 kg)
3 lb	1500 g (1.5 kg)
4 lb	2000 g (2 kg)

Key: oz = ounce; lb = pound;
g = gram; kg = kilogram.

Imperial Liquid Measures	Cup Measures	Metric Liquid Measures
1 fl oz		30 ml
2 fl oz	¼ cup	
3 fl oz		100 ml
4 fl oz (¼ pint US)	½ cup	
5 fl oz (¼ pint imp.)		150 ml
6 fl oz	¾ cup	
8 fl oz (½ pint US)	1 cup	250 ml
10 fl oz (½ pint imp.)	1¼ cups	
12 fl oz	1½ cups	
14 fl oz	1¾ cups	
16 fl oz (1 pint US)	2 cups	500 ml
20 fl oz (1 pint imp.)	2½ cups	

Key: fl oz = fluid ounce: ml = millilitre.

Oven Temperature Guide

The Celsius and Fahrenheit temperatures in the chart below relate to most electric ovens. Decrease by 10°C or 25°F for gas ovens or refer to the manufacturer's temperature guide. For temperatures below 160°C (325°F), do not decrease the given temperature.

Description of oven	Celsius °C	Fahrenheit °F	Gas Mark
Cool	100	200	¼
Very Slow	120	250	½
Slow	150	300	2
Moderately Slow	160	325	3
Moderate	180	350	4
Moderately Hot	190	375	5
Hot	200	400	6
Very Hot	230	450	8

Equivalent Terms

Most culinary terms in the English-speaking world can cross national borders without creating havoc in the kitchen. Nevertheless, local usage can produce some problems. The following list contains names of ingredients, equipment and cookery terms that are used in this book, but which may not be familiar to all readers.

Used in this book	Also known as
baking powder	double-acting baking powder
baking tray	baking sheet
bicarbonate of soda	baking soda
biscuits	cookies
boiler chicken	stewing chicken
pepper, red or green	sweet or bell pepper, capsicum
cornflour	cornstarch
desiccated coconut	shredded coconut
eggplant	aubergine
fillet (of meat)	tenderloin
frying pan	skillet
glace (fruits)	candied
grill/griller	broil/broiler
hard-boiled egg	hard-cooked egg
mincer	grinder
okra	gumbo, ladies' fingers
pastry	pie crust
pinch (of salt)	dash
plain flour	all-purpose flour
sieve	strain/strainer
(to) sift	(to) strain
spring onions	scallions, green onions
stone, seed, pip	pit
(to) whisk	(to) whip, beat
zucchini	courgettes

18

Foreground: Stuffed Peppers with Nogada Sauce and garnish *(Chillies Rellenos en Nogada),* recipe on page 45. Background: Blanched peppers and meat stuffing, prior to cooking.

Soups

The typical Latin American meal often begins with a soup and many of them, served with bread, are often substantial enough to be a stew. People in villages, rural areas and large cities accept nourishing soups as an essential part of their diet, and beans and lentils are often used, as well as potatoes and, according to availability, the more exotic vegetables such as avocados and coconut. When meat is scarce,

as it frequently is, the proportion of rice, beans, pasta or vegetables is increased.

Many of the soups in this section may be served as full meals, and I have included suggestions for accompaniments and wine. Other soups are lighter — the avocado, coconut, beetroot and pumpkin soups make an excellent prelude to almost any main course.

Beef Pastries *(Empanadas Cordobesas)*, recipe on page 46.

21

COCONUT SOUP
SOPA DE COCO

Serves: 6
Cooking time: 20 minutes

2 tablespoons cornflour (cornstarch)
2 cups milk
1 carton 250 g (8 oz) creamed coconut
3 cups chicken consommé or stock
1 onion, peeled and grated
salt
ground nutmeg
1 cup cream

Garnishes (optional):
prawns
cooked fish, flaked
spring onions (scallions)
sweet corn kernels
ham, diced
cashews, roasted and chopped

If creamed coconut is difficult to obtain, substitute 2½ cups of coconut milk (page 50) for the milk and creamed coconut.

Blend cornflour with a little of the milk. Heat together the remainder of the milk, creamed coconut, consommé or stock, onion, salt and nutmeg to taste. When almost boiling add the blended cornflour and stir with a wooden spoon until smooth and thickened. Add the cream and reheat but do not boil. Serve in bowls with a dash of nutmeg on top.

To round out this soup into a meal, serve a selection of the suggested garnishes. A dry sherry is best with this soup.

PORK AND CHILLI SOUP
AJI DE CERDO

This soup is really a hearty meal, but it is served in soup bowls, hence its name.

Serves: 6
Cooking time: 1 hour

1 tablespoon oil
1 kg (2 lb) boneless lean pork, cubed
1 large onion, sliced
1 tablespoon ground cummin
2 teaspoons salt
freshly ground black pepper
2 dried hot red chillies, crushed
2 cloves garlic, crushed
5 cups water
4 medium potatoes, peeled and quartered
1 x 500 g (16 oz) can corn kernels
2 tablespoons green pepper, chopped
¼ cup lemon juice
parsley, chopped

Heat the oil in a large, heavy-based saucepan and brown the pork. Add the onion, cummin, salt, pepper and chillies and stir for 2 minutes. Add garlic and the water, cover and simmer for 30 minutes. Add the potatoes and continue cooking till they are tender. Mix in the corn kernels, green pepper and lemon juice and reheat to boiling. Check the seasoning and ladle into soup bowls. Sprinkle fresh, chopped parsley over each serving.

Serve with plenty of fresh bread, a slaw of cabbage, onion and red apple, and beer.

SEAFOOD SOUP
SOPA LEAO VELLOSO

This soup is a full meal. It was originally created by a Brazilian diplomat many years ago.

Serves: 8-10
Cooking time: 1½ hours

1 x 2 kg (4 lb) mulloway, snapper or sea bass
4 litres (8 pints) water
salt
bunch of herbs
2 dozen mussels *or* oysters, scrubbed
500 g (1 lb) prawns
3 cloves garlic, crushed
2 teaspoons coriander seeds, crushed
1 tablespoon salt
1 cup spring onions (scallions)
1 cup parsley, chopped
3 tomatoes, peeled and chopped
cayenne pepper
2 tablespoons butter
500 g (1 lb) crab or lobster meat
½ cup dry white wine
3 egg yolks (optional)
2 teaspoons lemon juice (optional)

Clean and scale the fish and cut off the head. Slice the fish into steaks. Make a stock by heating the head in the salted water with herbs of your choice (e.g. parsley, bay leaf, fennel, etc). Cover and simmer for at least 1 hour. Remove the fish head and herbs and if there is any edible meat from the head set it aside.

If the mussels or oysters are fresh, cook them in the stock for 5 minutes or until the shells open. Separate the meat from the shells and shell and devein prawns. Strain the stock and add to it the garlic, coriander, salt, spring onions, parsley, tomatoes and cayenne pepper. Cover and simmer for 30 minutes. Heat butter and fry the fish steaks on both sides till cooked. Remove the skin and bones and discard. Cut the fish into chunks and add to the stock. Stir in mussels or oysters, prawns and crab or lobster meat. Pour a little of the stock into the fish frypan, add wine and bring to the boil. Scrape any drippings from the pan and pour them back into the stock. If you prefer a thicker broth, beat the egg yolks with the lemon juice and mix quickly into the soup. Check the seasoning, reheat the soup if necessary and serve in large bowls.

Plenty of fresh, french bread is essential with this soup. Try a salad of avocado slices with onion rings, tossed with lemon juice and pepper. The soup is worthy of a good, dry champagne.

THICK BEAN AND VEGETABLE SOUP
ENSOPADO COM FEIJAO
E LEGUMES   *BRAZIL*

Serves: 6
Cooking time: 1½ hours

2 cups dried haricot or navy beans
hot water to cover
250 g (8 oz) small onions, unpeeled
2 parsnips
2 tablespoons butter
1 kg (2 lb) lean, boneless pork
1 cup water
½ cup dry white wine
2 cups peeled tomatoes
2 bay leaves
1 teaspoon basil
salt
pepper

Garnish:
lemon peel, grated

Place the beans in a large bowl and cover with hot water. Soak for 1 hour, then drain and cover with fresh cold water in a large fireproof casserole. Boil until the beans are partially cooked but not yet soft (about 30-40 minutes). Drop the onions, with their skins on, into a pot of boiling water. Leave for a minute, then drain, cool in water and drain again. Peel the onions. Scrape the parsnips and slice thinly. Heat the butter, sauté the pork until browned and add it to the beans. In the same pan, sauté the onions and parsnips and add them to the beans. Add the water and wine to the same pan and bring to the boil. Simmer for a minute then add to the beans. Add the tomatoes with their juice, bay leaves and basil. Combine well by mixing lightly with a wooden spoon, cover with a lid and simmer over low heat for 45 minutes. Serve in bowls, garnished with grated lemon peel.

Serve with dark rye bread, sliced cucumbers in sour cream and light beer.

AVOCADO SOUP
SOPA DE AGUACATE   *MEXICO*

Serves: 6

3 large, ripe avocados
1 tablespoon lemon juice
4 cups chicken stock, chilled
salt
1 clove garlic, crushed
few drops Tabasco sauce (optional)
2 cups cream

Garnish:
lemon slices *or* avocado slices

Peel avocados, remove seeds and place in blender with lemon juice. Remove all fat from chilled chicken stock and add to blender with garlic and Tabasco. Blend until smooth and stir in the cream. If you do not have a blender, mash the avocado with a fork and add the other ingredients while stirring. Chill and serve garnished with slices of lemon or avocado.

Fried bread or corn chips are good accompaniments for this refreshing soup, as well as a dry sherry.

CHICKEN AND RICE SOUP
CANJA

Serves: 8
Cooking time: 1 hour

1 1.5 kg (3 lb) chicken
1 tablespoon butter
1 tablespoon oil
2 cups peeled tomatoes (fresh or canned),
  chopped
water to cover chicken
2 onions, peeled and quartered
2 tablespoons parsley *or* coriander, chopped
salt
ground pepper
1 cup short grain rice
½ cup ham *or* smoked tongue, chopped
fresh parsley

Cut the chicken into pieces then brown in the heated butter and oil. Add the tomatoes and cook for a minute. Cover the chicken with water and add the onions, parsley, pepper and salt. Bring to the boil, cover and simmer for 30 minutes. Remove the chicken, and when cool, remove skin and cut meat from the bones. Cut the meat into very fine strips. Strain the stock and make up to 8 cups. Add rice to the reheated stock together with the chicken meat and ham. Simmer until the rice is cooked. Serve garnished with fresh chopped parsley.

Accompany with garlic bread and a platter of stuffed eggs with dill mayonnaise. A few drops of Tabasco sauce may be added at the table. A chilled, dry Chablis would go well with this soup.

BAHIAN SOUP
SOPA BAHIANO

This soup comes from north eastern Brazil where the cuisine has a strong African influence.

Serves: 6
Cooking time: 1½ hours

2 meaty ham bones, each about 1 kg (2 lb)
5 cups water
1 onion, peeled
4 cloves
4 allspice berries
3 sweet potatoes, peeled and sliced
½ teaspoon dried thyme
ground pepper
3 plantains *or* firm bananas
¼ cup spring onions (scallions), sliced

Place ham bones in a large pan with water (it may be necessary to cut the bones to fit). Tie the onion, cloves and allspice in a muslin (cheesecloth) bag and add to the pan. Bring to the boil, cover and simmer for 1 hour. Remove and discard the muslin bag. Remove the bones and cut off all the meat. Discard the bones and rind. Add the meat back to the stock together with the sweet potatoes, thyme and pepper. Simmer for 20 minutes and lightly stir in the bananas and spring onions (scallions). Reheat gently and serve in soup bowls.

Serve with a platter of sliced salami, tomatoes and onion with oil and lemon dressing. Caraway seed or rye bread is a good accompaniment.

PUMPKIN SOUP
API ZAPALLO   *ARGENTINA*

Serves: 6
Cooking time: 1 hour

2 kg (4 lb) pumpkin, peeled and cut into pieces
salt
250 g (8 oz) fat bacon, chopped
2 onions, chopped finely
ground chillies to taste
1 teaspoon ground cummin
300 g (10 oz) grated cheese
chopped parsley

Place the pumpkin into a clay casserole with salt and just enough water to prevent burning (it is traditional to cook it in a clay pot). Cook until the pumpkin is very tender and drain off any excess water (about 40 minutes). Mash well with a fork. Place the bacon into a cold pan, then place over moderate heat so that it will render the bacon fat, and cook the bacon till crisp. Stir in the onions and fry for a minute. Add the contents of the pan to the casserole with the pumpkin and stir well with a wooden spoon. Add the chillies, cummin and cheese and mix over low heat until very hot. Serve in bowls garnished with finely chopped parsley.

This soup may be thinned with cream or milk if you prefer.

Serve as an entrée if a light meal follows, or as a meal with the addition of salad and a good rye or wholemeal bread. Serve with sherry or a not too dry white wine.

CORN SOUP WITH PRAWNS
SOPA DE MILHO COM CAMARAO   *BRAZIL*

Serves: 6
Cooking time: 25 minutes

1 kg (2 lb) small cooked prawns
salt
ground black pepper
1 clove garlic, crushed
4 coriander seeds, crushed
5 cups chicken *or* fish stock
2 x 440 g (16 oz) cans cream-style corn
2 onions, finely chopped
2 tablespoons butter
2 egg yolks
1 tablespoon lemon juice

Garnish:
whole prawns

Shell and devein the prawns, then season with the salt, pepper, garlic and coriander. Let stand 10 minutes, then chop the prawns, reserving a few whole for garnish. Heat the stock and add the corn. Simmer for 15 minutes. Fry the onion in the butter and add the prawns. Toss to heat the prawns and remove from heat. Pass the corn and stock through a strainer into the prawn and onion mixture. Reheat but do not boil. Beat the egg yolks and lemon juice with a whisk or fork and blend quickly into the hot soup. Garnish each serving with whole prawns.

Serve with hot sesame rolls and a bowl of avocados, seasoned with salt, pepper, lemon juice, Tabasco and sour cream. Add a spoonful of the avocado as you eat. Serve it with a rosé.

BEETROOT SOUP
SOPA DE BETERRABA

Serves: 6
Cooking time: 50 minutes

625 g (1¼ lb) fresh beetroot (beets)
water to cover beetroot
8 cups beef stock
1 leek, sliced
1 x 470 g (16 oz) can artichoke hearts
2 tablespoons madeira wine *or* sherry
salt to taste
ground pepper
500 g (1 lb) smoked beef, diced

Garnishes:
½ cup cream
2 teaspoons lemon juice
½ teaspoon horseradish
  ***or* 1 teaspoon prepared horseradish**
chopped parsley

Trim beetroot, cut into pieces and cook in water for 30 minutes. Drain and set aside. Heat 4 cups of stock and when boiling, drop in the leek. Cook 10 minutes, then remove with a slotted spoon, reserving the stock. Place the beetroot, leek and drained artichokes into a blender and blend until smooth, or pass through a food mill. Add the purée to the extra 4 cups of stock and add to the hot stock remaining in pan. Reheat and stir in the wine, salt, pepper and beef. Combine the cream, lemon juice and horseradish until smooth. Ladle the hot soup into bowls and garnish with a generous spoonful of the horseradish cream and chopped parsley.

Serve with a good rye or wholemeal bread and an onion salad — consisting of whole baby onions, parboiled and tossed with oil, lemon juice, garlic and basil. I prefer a white wine with this dish but a red wine is equally suitable.

PEANUT SOUP
(SOPA DE AMENDOIM)

BOLIVIA

Serves: 6
Cooking time: 20 minutes

60 g (2 oz) peanuts, ground
4 tablespoons rice flour
1 egg
2 tablespoons milk
5 cups chicken stock
1 cup cooked chicken, diced
parsley, chopped, for garnish

Mix the ground peanuts and rice flour in a small bowl. Beat the egg and milk together lightly and add to the peanuts and flour. Beat well and set aside. Bring the chicken stock to the boil in a saucepan with a well fitting lid. Drop the peanut mixture into the stock, using a teaspoon. Cover the pan and simmer over low heat for 15 minutes. Add the chicken meat and reheat. Serve immediately, garnished with chopped parsley.

SPINACH SOUP
(SOPA DE ESPINACAS)

VENEZUELA

Serves: 6
Cooking time: 30 minutes

500 g (1 lb) spinach
5 cups chicken stock
2 leeks, sliced
1 onion, chopped
250 g (8 oz) okra
pepper
salt
250 g (8 oz) ham, chopped

Wash the spinach and chop it coarsely. Place it in a saucepan with the chicken stock, leeks and onion. Bring to the boil and simmer for 15 minutes. Remove stems from the okra and add them to the soup in the saucepan. Add pepper and salt to taste, cover and simmer for 15 minutes. Add the ham, reheat, and serve immediately.

28

Sauces

Piquant, spicy sauces are important components of many Latin American dishes. In fact, many traditional dishes are not complete without them.

The sauces given in this section are very versatile, and are intended to be used for main courses or desserts. The pepper and lemon sauce from Brazil (page 30) is an accompaniment to many dishes, and I have had it served with *feijoada* (page 66) and *vatapá* (page 96).

AVOCADO SAUCE
SALSA GUASACACA
VENEZUELA, MEXICO

Yield: 1½ cups

1 large avocado
1 tablespoon lemon juice
¼ teaspoon dried, hot chillies, crushed
  or 3 drops Tabasco sauce
salt
pepper
1 tomato, peeled
¼ cup parsley, chopped
½ teaspoon ground coriander
1 tablespoon oil
1 tablespoon vinegar
1 tablespoon chopped green olives (optional)

Cut the avocado in half, remove the seed and scoop out the flesh. Chop or mash roughly and mix in the lemon juice. Add the chillies, salt, pepper and chopped tomato. Blend well and fold in parsley, coriander, oil, vinegar and olives. Cover and refrigerate until required.

Serve with fish or meats.

TOMATO AND CASHEW SAUCE
MOLHO DE TOMATE E CASTANYAS DE CAJU
BRAZIL

Yield: 1½ cups
Cooking time: 5-10 minutes

1 tablespoon butter
1 cup tomatoes, peeled and chopped
½ cup cream
¼ cup ground cashews
salt
pepper

Melt butter, add tomatoes and cook until soft, (about 5 minutes). Add cream and nuts and season to taste. Reheat and serve with chicken, fish pork or vegetables.

PEPPER AND LEMON SAUCE
MOLHO DE PIMENTA E LIMAO
BRAZIL

Yield: ½ cup

3 or 4 tiny hot chillies, fresh or dried
½ teaspoon salt
1 clove garlic, crushed
1 onion, quartered
½ cup lemon juice

Purée chillies, salt, crushed garlic and quartered onion in a food mill or blender. Add lemon juice and allow to stand for 1-2 hours. The sauce can be kept in a covered jar in the refrigerator for a short period, but will ferment if allowed to stand too long.

Serve with *feijoada* (page 66) and *vatapá* (page 96).

ALMOND SAUCE
SALSA DE ALMENDRAS   *ARGENTINA*

Yield: 2¼ cups
Cooking time: 15 minutes

2 tablespoons butter
2 tablespoons flour
2 cups chicken stock
¼ cup almonds, chopped
¼ cup raisins
salt
pepper
2 teaspoons lemon juice

Melt butter and add flour. Blend well and cook for 2 minutes. Add stock and cook over low heat, stirring constantly until thick and bubbling (about 10 minutes). Add almonds, raisins, salt, pepper and lemon juice.

Serve with fish, chicken or pork.

PRAWN AND COCONUT SAUCE
MOLHO DE CAMARAO E COCO   *BRAZIL*

Yield: 3 cups
Cooking time: 15 minutes

1 tablespoon butter
1 tablespoon flour
1½ cups coconut milk (page 50)
1 tablespoon butter
1 tablespoon onion, chopped
¾ cup shelled prawns
1 cup tomato sauce

Melt butter, stir in flour and cook for 1 minute. Add coconut milk and simmer 10 minutes. Put aside. Sauté the onion in the other tablespoon of butter and stir in the prawns and tomato sauce. Combine both mixtures and season.

Serve with fish.

ORANGE SAUCE
MOLHO DE GELEIA DE LARANJA   *BRAZIL*

Yield: 2 cups
Cooking time: 10-15 minutes

1 cup orange marmalade
1 tablespoon sugar
½ cup water
juice of 1 orange
3 teaspoons arrowroot
1 tablespoon orange liqueur (e.g. Cointreau)

Heat the marmalade, sugar and water together in a small saucepan. Blend the orange juice with the arrowroot and stir into the hot mixture. Stir with a wooden spoon until thick and clear (about 10 minutes). Remove from heat and add the orange liqueur.

Serve hot or cold with desserts.

31

RED CHILLI SAUCE
(SALSA DE CHILI ROJO)   *MEXICO*

Yield: 2 cups
Cooking time: 10-15 minutes

5 small hot chillies, fresh or dried
2 tablespoons boiling water
1 clove garlic
3 onions, chopped
1½ cups peeled tomatoes
½ teaspoon cumin
2 tablespoons oil
2 tablespoons vinegar
salt
pepper

Remove stems from chillies and break chillies open. Remove the seeds and cover the chillies with the boiling water for 5 minutes. Place them in a blender with the garlic, onion, tomatoes and cumin and blend until smooth. Heat the oil in a saucepan and add the chilli sauce. Cook over medium heat for 10-15 minutes, add the vinegar and season to taste with the salt and pepper. Cool and store in the refrigerator until required.

NOTE: Serve with *tortillas* (page 54), *tacos* (page 57) or meat dishes.

CHILEAN SAUCE
(PEBRE)   *CHILE*

Yield: 1½ cups

3 small hot chillies, fresh or dried
1 tablespoon boiling water
1 tablespoon oil
½ cup water
1 tablespoon vinegar
2 onions, sliced
½ cup chopped fresh coriander or parsley
1 teaspoon oregano
1 teaspoon salt

Remove stems from chillies and break chillies open. Remove seeds and cover with the boiling water for 5 minutes. Place them in a blender with all the remaining ingredients and blend for a few seconds. This sauce may be stored in the refrigerator until required.

NOTE: Serve at room temperature to accompany roast or grilled meats.

Entrées and Accompaniments

Latin American cooks choose entrées and accompaniments to main courses with great care. Of course, they must consider what fruits and vegetables are seasonally available, and which are freshest at the market. Tradition also plays a role, for certain dishes demand certain accompaniments. For example, the *feijoada* of Brazil is not considered complete without rice, kale, *farofa* (page 44), orange slices and white rum.

However, certain ingredients are always available. Mexico, Chile and Brazil use a lot of beans in their cooking, and beans are served daily with lunch and sometimes with dinner. This section contains a delicious recipe for re-fried beans (page 49).

The vegetable and cheese tortes (pages 53 and 34) may be served with several other dishes at an informal lunch or dinner gathering, rather like our buffet-style meals where several dishes and accompaniments are placed on the table at once.

No section on entrées and accompaniments would be complete without at least a few *tortilla* recipes. By tradition, the *tortilla* forms the basic accompaniment to Mexican meals. These thin, baked 'pancakes' made from corn dough can be served with fillings or toppings as a complete meal. Variants of the *tortilla* —

enchiladas, tacos and *tostados* — are popular throughout Latin America. *Tamales* are similar, but the corn dough is steamed in corn husks rather than baked.

Corn dough is the basic ingredient in the *tortilla*. Dehydrated *masa* flour may also be used, or fresh, prepared dough for *tortilla*-making may be available. If it is not possible to buy *masa harina* in your area, do not attempt to use cornflour (cornstarch) or cornmeal (polenta) as these are not suitable substitutes. If you cannot buy *masa* flour, try the recipe for wheat tortillas (page 58). These are similar to the *tortillas* made in the north of Mexico.

Beef, pork or chicken may be substituted for the suggested fillings. *Tostados* or corn chips, which are often accompaniments for drinks, are made by frying whole or quartered *tortillas* in deep, hot oil until crisp. *Tostados* may be served with dips or spreads.

Finally, drinks are as important an accompaniment to meals as are vegetables, rice or *tortillas*. Whether they choose the excellent wines of Chile or Argentina, the *sangria* of Argentina and Mexico or the *cachaca* of Brazil — or even fresh fruit juices — no Latin Americans eat without drinking or drink without eating.

CHEESE TORTE
TORTA DE QUEIJO or TORTA DE QUESO

While this torte is more a supper or lunch dish rather than an accompaniment, it is difficult to classify. This delicious short pastry is one of the simplest I have encountered.

Serves: 6
Cooking time: 30 minutes
Oven temperature: 180°C (350°F)

Pastry:
½ cup cream
4 tablespoons oil *or* melted lard
1 teaspoon baking powder
1 cup plain flour

Filling:
1 cup cheddar cheese, grated
1 cup parmesan cheese, grated
1 cup Gouda cheese, grated
4 eggs
½ cup cream
salt
pepper

Place the cream, dripping and baking powder in a bowl. Gradually add the flour, mixing it in with the back of a fork until the pastry comes together into a soft but firm dough. Line a 30 cm (12 in) pie dish or flan tin with the pastry. There is no need to roll it, just press the dough into the ungreased dish with your fingers. Spread all the cheese over the pastry. Beat the eggs lightly with the cream, salt and pepper. Pour over the cheese and bake in a moderate oven until the egg is set and golden (about 30 minutes).

This is a perfect late night supper. Prepare it earlier with the cheese in the pastry shell and refrigerate. When you return, whisk the eggs and cream and pour over it. Leave it to bake while you organise drinks.

SPINACH SAVOURY
ESPINAFRE SABOROSO

Serves: 4
Cooking time: 10-15 minutes
Oven temperature: 220°C (425°F)

2 cups spinach, cooked and drained
1 tablespoon lemon juice
¼ cup cream
salt
pepper
½ teaspoon nutmeg or mace
3 tablespoons parmesan cheese, grated

Garnishes:
2 tablespoons cooked, crisp bacon
1 hard boiled egg

Chop the spinach roughly and add the lemon juice. Place in a small, greased casserole and pour over the combined cream, salt, pepper and nutmeg. Sprinkle with the cheese and bake in a hot oven for 10-15 minutes. To serve, garnish with the crumbled bacon and finely chopped egg.

MARINATED FISH
CEVICHE

Just a note for those wary of eating 'raw' fish: marinating in lemon or lime juice has the same effect as cooking. The fish becomes firm and white with the appearance of cooked fish. This dish is usually served as an entrée or a luncheon dish.

Serves: 6

1 cup each lime juice and lemon juice
   or 2 cups lemon juice
2 onions, sliced thinly
1 clove garlic, crushed
½ teaspoon dried hot chillies, crushed
freshly ground black pepper
1 teaspoon salt
1 kg (2 lb) white fish fillets (snapper or sea bass) cut into 25 mm (1 in) pieces

Garnishes:
lettuce leaves
onion rings
½ sweet red pepper (capsicum),
   cut into strips
cobs of corn, cooked and cut in half
sweet potato or yams, cooked and sliced

Mix the fruit juices, onion, garlic, chillies, pepper and salt in a bowl. Place fish in a shallow glass or ceramic dish and pour this mixture over it. The fish must be covered; if not, add more fruit juice. Cover the dish closely and refrigerate for several hours until fish looks 'cooked'. Serve on lettuce leaves garnished with onion rings and very thin strips of red capsicum.

In Peru, sea bass is used, and this dish is traditionally served with sliced, cooked sweet potato and corn on the cob, both cold.

PRAWN COCKTAIL
COQUETEL DE CAMARAO

Serves: 6

1 kg (2 lb) prawns
1 onion, grated
1 cup tomato sauce
1 teaspoon dry mustard
2 teaspoons Worcestershire sauce
1 tablespoon lemon juice
Tabasco (optional)
½ cup celery, sliced thinly
1 tablespoon brandy or cognac
¾ cup mayonnaise
shredded lettuce
lemon wedges

Shell the prawns and cut in half, or leave whole if they are small. Reserve some to garnish the side of the glass. Mix the prawns with the onion, tomato sauce, mustard, Worcestershire sauce, lemon juice, Tabasco, celery and brandy. Adding enough mayonnaise to make a thick creamy mixture. Place a layer of finely shredded lettuce in each glass and top with the prawn mixture. Garnish with whole prawns and lemon wedges.

Serve with fingers of buttered wholemeal bread and a dry white wine.

CODFISH BALLS
BOLINHOS DE BACALHAU

Despite the abundance of fresh fish in Brazil, one of the most popular seafoods is the dried salt cod (bacalhau). This is served in countless ways, restricted only by the cook's creativity. The dried, salted fish must be pre-soaked and simmered to remove the excess salt before it is used for cooking. One particularly delicious dish is bacalhau na brasa, *freshened cod grilled over hot coals and brushed with oil and seasonings. Another favourite is the following recipe; these codfish balls are usually served with drinks rather than as a meal.*

Yield: 20-24
Cooking time: 10 minutes

500 g (1 lb) dried, salt cod
1 tablespoon oil
1 tablespoon butter
½ cup parsley, chopped
½ cup spring onions (scallions), chopped
½ teaspoon pepper *or* **paprika**
2 eggs
2 cups mashed potatoes
½ cup plain flour
½ cup milk
oil for frying

Cut the cod into about 6 pieces and cover with cold water. Soak for several hours or overnight, changing the water as often as possible. Drain, cover with fresh water and bring to the boil. Simmer for 10 minutes, then drain and remove any skin and bones. Heat the oil and butter over a medium heat and sauté the fish with the parsley, spring onions and pepper. Cook until the fish will flake easily with a fork. Remove from the heat and pull the fish into shreds with a fork, add the eggs, mashed potato and flour. Blend together well and add enough milk to make a smooth but still firm mixture. Allow to cool, then roll into balls about 5 cm (2 in) in diameter, drop into deep hot oil and fry for 8-10 minutes or until golden brown. Drain on absorbent paper and serve hot.

Squares of Vegetable Torte *(Torta de Legumes)*, recipe on page 53, topped with Corn and Ham Cupcakes *(Quindins de Milho Verde e Presunto)*, recipe on page 52.

STUFFED CRABS
CASQUINHOS DE CARANGUEJO

In many parts of Latin America, it is customary to serve delicious little savoury nibbles with pre-dinner drinks, and many require as much preparation as the meal. In Brazil these are known as salgadinhos. *The following recipe is one of these, but as it needs to be eaten with a small fork or spoon, it is suitable as an entrée.*

Serves: 6
Cooking time: 10 minutes
Oven temperature: 220°C (425°F)

6 large sand crabs *or* 12 small coral crabs, cooked
¼ cup oil
3 cloves garlic, crushed
2 onions, chopped
½ cup tomatoes, peeled and chopped
salt
½ cup parsley, chopped
2 spring onions (scallions), sliced
¼ cup fresh coriander, chopped
½ teaspoon hot chilli powder
3 egg yolks
1 cup coconut milk (page 50) *or* 1 tablespoon creamed coconut in 1 cup milk
60 g (2 oz) roasted cashews, ground
60 g (2 oz) roasted peanuts, ground
3 slices bread
3 tablespoons milk
1 egg, beaten
packaged breadcrumbs

Garnishes:
stuffed olives
hard boiled egg

Remove all meat from the crab shells, taking care not to break the backs. Reserve the crab shell backs after washing. Heat the oil and add the garlic, onions, tomatoes, salt, parsley, spring onions, coriander and chilli powder. Stir well and cook for 5 minutes, then add the crab meat. Remove the pan from the heat and add the egg yolks, coconut milk, cashews and peanuts. Soak the sliced bread in the milk and add. Return to low heat and mix carefully with a wooden spoon until the mixture becomes creamy. If necessary, sprinkle with a little flour and stir till thickened. Season with salt and pepper and place in a bowl to cool. Fill the shells with the crab cream, brush the base with beaten egg and sprinkle with breadcrumbs. Place in a hot oven for 10 minutes or until browned. Garnish with slices of hard boiled egg and stuffed olives.

Serve accompanied with rings of fried peppers (capsicum) and a fruity, dry white wine.

Foreground: Seasoned Puréed Corn, steamed in corn husks *(Humitas en Chala)*, see page 54. Background: Seasoned Puréed Corn *(Humitas)*, recipe on page 54.

PASTRIES WITH CREAM CHEESE
PASTEISINHOS COM CREME DE QUEIJO   *BRAZIL*

The pastries of Brazil, Argentina and Chile are so delicious that I have included as many as possible. You will find them described as empanadas, empadas, empadinhas, pastels *or* pasteisinhos. *The variety of filling is so wide, particularly in Brazil, that it is impossible to include them all. The little pastries below are particularly suitable to serve with pre-dinner drinks or as an entrée.*

Yield: 18-20
Cooking time: 15 minutes
Oven temperature: 200°C (400°F)

Pastry:
½ cup butter
1 teaspoon salt
½ cup ricotta cheese
1 cup flour

Filling:
125 g (4 oz) cheese spread

To brush over:
1 egg yolk
1 teaspoon oil

Cream the butter with the salt. Press the ricotta through a sieve and add it. Mix well with a fork, and continue mixing as you add the flour, a little at a time until the dough does not stick to the hands; if necessary add a little more flour. Cover with plastic wrap and place in the refrigerator for a few hours or overnight. Roll our thinly on a lightly floured board and use a glass to cut small rounds about 8 cm (3 in) in diameter. Place a teaspoon of the cheese spread on the pastry and fold in half. Crimp the edges well with a fork and place them on a greased baking sheet. Brush over with the egg yolk and oil mixture and bake in a moderately hot oven until browned (about 10-15 minutes).

STUFFED APPLES
MACAS RECHEADAS   *BRAZIL*

Serves: 6

6 red apples
lemon juice

Sauce:
1 cup cream
2 teaspoons lemon juice
½ teaspoon mustard powder
salt
pepper

Filling:
1½ cups mixed vegetables
any mixture of cooked vegetables such as carrot, potato *or* tomato, leeks, capsicum, peas, onion and parsley.

Cut the top off the apples and hollow them out, leaving a shell of about 2 cm (¾ in) in thickness. Sprinkle with lemon juice. Mix all the sauce ingredients and combine with your choice of vegetables. Fill the cavities and garnish with parsley.

This dish is a good accompaniment to cold roast pork, chicken or turkey.

FRIED CHOKO BALLS
BOLINHAS DE CHUCHU FRITOS

This is an unusual way of serving the humble choko, and is delicious with pre-dinner drinks or as a vegetable accompaniment to the main course. In that case garnish with finely sliced spring onions or chopped parsley.

Serves: 4-6
Cooking time: 5 minutes

3 chokos (*chayotes*)
2 tablespoons flour
1 egg, beaten
packaged breadcrumbs
oil for frying

Peel the chokos, remove seed and use a melon baller to scoop them out. Wash the balls and dry them with kitchen towels. Dust with the flour, then pass them through the beaten egg and roll in breadcrumbs. Deep fry in hot oil until golden brown. Drain well and serve immediately.

BAKED ORANGES
LARANJAS GRATINADAS

Serves: 8
Cooking time: 20 minutes
Oven temperature: 220°C (425°F)

4 oranges
1 tablespoon butter
1 tablespoon flour
salt
pepper
½ cup dry white wine
¼ cup mushrooms, chopped
1 tablespoon tomato sauce
1 cup cream
2 eggs
⅓ cup parmesan cheese, grated.

Cut the oranges in half and remove the pulp, keeping the skins intact. Chop the pulp and reserve 1 cup, without any membranes. Heat the butter, blend in the flour and allow to brown slightly. Add salt and pepper and stir in the wine, a little at a time, stirring constantly. Add the mushrooms, tomato sauce and cream. Mix well and add the orange pulp. Fill the orange skins with this mixture and sprinkle with a little basil if you wish. Beat the eggs and pour over the mixture in the skins. Sprinkle liberally with parmesan cheese and place in a hot oven until well browned (about 20 minutes). Serve immediately.

Serve with roast duck, chicken, pork or fish.

SMALL MEAT PIES
EMPADINHAS DE CARNE   *BRAZIL*

These little pies are delicious with drinks, or they may be made slightly larger for individual.entrées. I have included only the meat filling, but they are often made with leftover cooked chicken or prawns. The pastry is simple, short and needs no rolling. Simply press into patty tins.

Yield: 1 dozen patty size pies
Cooking time: 20 minutes
Oven temperature: 180°C (350°F)

Pastry:
¼ cup cream
2 tablespoons oil
1 teaspoon baking powder
½ teaspoon salt
¾ cup plain flour

Filling:
1 tablespoon oil
250 g (8 oz) minced steak
1 onion, chopped
1 small potato, diced
salt
pepper
½ teaspoon paprika
½ teaspoon oregano
½ cup stock *or* water
1 teaspoon flour
2 hard boiled eggs
1 green olive for each pie

Topping:
½ cup cheese, grated
1 egg, beaten
1 tablespoon milk
1 tablespoon cream

Place the cream, oil, baking powder and salt in a bowl. Blend in the flour gradually with a fork, until the mixture is soft but comes together into a ball. It should not stick to your hands; add more flour if necessary to prevent sticking. If possible, stand the pastry aside for 15-20 minutes. Break off small pieces of pastry about the size of a walnut and press into ungreased patty tins. To prepare the filling, heat the oil and brown the meat and onions. Add the potato, salt, pepper, paprika, oregano and the stock or water. Simmer for 10 minutes then sprinkle over the flour and stir in well. Cook for a minute longer. Remove from the heat and add the chopped eggs. Allow to cool. Pour filling into each pie until ¾ full. Top each pie with a seeded olive and sprinkle over a little cheese. Combine the. beaten egg, milk and cream. Pour about 1 teaspoon of egg mixture on top of each pie and bake in a moderate oven for 20 minutes, or until the filling has set and browned.

STUFFED CUCUMBERS
PEPINOS RELLENOS   *MEXICO, BRAZIL*

Serves: 6

2 cucumbers
salt
125 g (4 oz) cream cheese
1 tablespoon onion, chopped
½ teaspoon salt
pepper
½ teaspoon ground chillies

Cut one end from cucumbers and carefully scoop out all the seeds and soft centre. Sprinkle inside with salt and leave upside down to drain. Soften cheese and blend with the onion, salt, pepper and chilli, Dry cucumbers with kitchen paper towels and fill with the cheese mixture. Cover with plastic wrap and refrigerate until required. Score the skin lightly with a fork and cut into 1 cm (½ in) slices.

Serve with cold meats.

BASIC BRAZILIAN RICE
ARROZ SIMPLES   *BRAZIL*

Serves: 6
Cooking time: 30 minutes

2 tablespoons oil
1 onion, chopped
2 cloves garlic, crushed
2 cups short grain rice
4 cups water *or* **stock**
salt

Heat oil and sauté the onion and garlic, then add the washed rice and cook for a few minutes, but do not brown. Add the hot water or stock and salt to taste. Bring to the boil, cover, and reduce heat to very low. Simmer until all liquid is absorbed (about 20 minutes). Remove from heat and let stand undisturbed with the lid on for 15-30 minutes. The steam in the saucepan will cause the grains to separate. Stir lightly with a fork and serve.

WHEATMEAL FAROFA

FAROFA DE TRIGO

Farofa in one form or another accompanies almost every Brazilian meal. Sometimes the untoasted manioc (bitter cassava) meal is served simply in a shaker at the table, but it is more often toasted in butter or oil with eggs, olives, bananas, bacon or onion added. The flour or meal of cassava may be difficult to find outside Latin America, but I have found this wheatmeal farofa to be quite successful.

Serves: 4
Cooking time 5-10 minutes

2 tablespoons butter
1 tablespoon oil
1 onion, chopped
1 clove garlic, crushed
2 cups wheatmeal
salt
½ teaspoon paprika
2 spring onions (scallions), chopped
2 tablespoons parsley, chopped
2 tablespoons green olives, chopped
2 hard-boiled eggs

Garnish:
roasted nuts

Heat the butter and oil over moderate heat and sauté the onion and garlic for 1 minute. Mix in the wheatmeal and stir with a wooden spoon until all the wheatmeal is coated with butter. Continue to stir for 5 minutes until the meal is lightly browned and toasted. Add salt and paprika, then stir in the spring onions, parsley, olives and sliced eggs.

Variation
Instead of the eggs and olives, substitute 2 bananas, sliced, and 2 tablespoons chopped ham.

This dish may be used to accompany barbecued steak, fish or chicken. The Brazilians frequently use it to stuff chicken or whole fish. If desired, garnish with roasted nuts.

STUFFED PEPPERS WITH NOGADA SAUCE
CHILLIES RELLENOS EN NOGADA   *MEXICO*

Serves: 6
Cooking time: 35 minutes

6 medium green peppers (capsicums)
boiling water to cover
2 tablespoons oil
500 g (1 lb) minced beef
175 g (6 oz) ham, finely chopped
1 clove garlic, crushed
1 small onion, chopped
1 cup peeled tomatoes, chopped
2 tablespoons vinegar
1 teaspoon ground cloves
1 teaspoon ground cinnamon
2 tablespoons raisins
2 tablespoons almonds, chopped
2 tablespoons stuffed olives, sliced
2 eggs
1 teaspoon salt
¼ cup plain flour
oil for frying

Sauce:
1 cup cream
¼ cup ground almonds
½ cup ground walnuts
1 teaspoon sugar
½ teaspoon salt

Garnish:
pomegranate seeds
   or finely chopped red pepper

Remove stems from peppers and discard seeds and membranes. Cover with boiling water and stand for 5 minutes. Drain and invert peppers onto kitchen towels to dry. Heat the oil and brown the beef. Add the ham, garlic and onion and stir over a medium heat for 5 minutes. Stir in the tomatoes, vinegar, cloves and cinnamon and cook for 30 minutes. Add the raisins, almonds and olives. Fill the peppers with the meat stuffing and pack it in well. Beat the eggs and blend in the salt and flour. Dry the skin of the peppers well and dip in the batter. Fry in deep, hot oil for about 5 minutes or until golden brown. Remove the peppers with a slotted spoon and drain well. To make the sauce, beat the cream until thick, and fold in the almonds, walnuts, sugar and salt. Top each pepper with sauce and garnish with pomegranate seeds or chopped red pepper.

The green, white and red colours of the peppers, sauce and garnish represent the Mexican flag.

BEEF PASTRIES
EMPANADAS CORDOBESAS

These beef pastries may be baked in the oven (al horno) *or deep fried* (fritas). *The ingredients vary from region to region. These beef pastries are typical of the Cordoba area, in the hills below the Argentine Andes.*

Serves: 6-8
Cooking time: 15 minutes

Pastry:
6 cups plain flour, sifted
1 cup butter *or* **dripping, melted**
salt
cold water to bind
1 egg, beaten

Filling:
½ cup oil *or* **dripping**
2 large onions, chopped
1 peeled tomato, chopped
½ cup sweet red pepper (capsicum)
1 kg (2 lb) round steak, cubed
½ cup parsley, chopped
1 large cooked potato, cubed
¼ cup plain flour
½ cup stock
2 hard-boiled eggs, chopped
½ cup seeded green olives, chopped
½ cup raisins
salt
chilli powder (optional)

Filling: Heat dripping and fry onions, tomato and capsicum. Remove from the heat, add steak, parsley, potato, flour and stock. Cook over a low heat until cooked through. Remove from heat and add the eggs, olives and raisins. Season with salt and chilli powder. When the mixture is cool fill the pastry cases.

Pastry: Make a well in the sifted flour and pour in the cooled, melted dripping or butter. Add salt and mix well. Add water as required to make a firm dough. Place dough on a floured table and kneed till smooth and pliable. Roll out and cut circles of dough about the size of a saucer. Place 2 tablespoons of filling in the centre of each circle. Moisten the edges of the pastry and join them together to form a half-moon shape. Press the edges together well and decorate them with a finger pattern or with a fork. Place on an ungreased baking tray, brush over with beaten egg and bake in a hot oven for 15 minutes.

46

RICE TO SERVE WITH CHICKEN OR ROLLED BEEF
RISOTTO PARA POLLO Y MATAMBRE   *LATIN AMERICA*

Serves: 6
Cooking time: 20-40 minutes

⅓ cup oil
2 cups long grain rice
1 onion, chopped
½ cup mushrooms, chopped
¼ teaspoon saffron
salt
4 cups chicken stock *or* beef stock

Heat butter in a casserole and sauté rice and onion until rice is opaque. Add the mushrooms and saffron and a little salt. Pour in the heated stock and bring to the boil. Lower the heat, cover the casserole and cook until liquid is absorbed (about 20 minutes). The chicken pieces or meat slices are usually added and cooked for 20 minutes longer (without lid). Add more stock if required.

AREQUIPA-STYLE POTATOES
PAPAS AREQUIPENA   *PERU*

Serves: 6
Cooking time: 15 minutes

½ cup peanuts, ground
¼ cup cream
¼ cup milk
⅓ cup peanut oil *or* ⅓ cup vegetable oil
salt
pepper
1½ teaspoons hot chillies, ground
1 small onion, peeled
½ cup Munster cheese, grated
    or ½ cup feta cheese, crumbled
1 kg (2 lb) potatoes
boiling salted water to cover potatoes

Garnishes:
hard boiled eggs
black olives

Put the peanuts, cream, milk, oil, salt, pepper, chillies, onion and cheese in a blender and mix at high speed for a few seconds until smooth. Pour into a jug. Peel and halve the potatoes, drop into boiling salted water and cook for 10-15 minutes until tender but not overcooked. Drain potatoes well and arrange them, cut side down, on a serving platter. Pour the sauce over them and garnish with sliced eggs and black olives.

LITTLE CHEESE BREADS
PAO DE QUEIJO MINEIRO

I used to make these frequently in Brazil, using cheese from the state of Minas Gerais and sour polvilho *flour from the tapioca plant. It is impossible to duplicate either of these ingredients, but I have had good results using the following method. The mixture can remain covered in the refrigerator for up to a week. Simply roll into balls and bake in the oven when you want them. The recipe can be doubled successfully.*

Yield: 2 dozen
Cooking time: 20-30 minutes
Oven temperature: 230°C (450°F)

2 cups tapioca flour
½ cup cold water
1 teaspoon salt
2 x 55 g (1¾ oz) eggs
½ cup lard or pork fat
2 cups Munster cheese, grated
   or 2 cups feta cheese, crumbled
½ cup water

Place the tapioca flour in a bowl and pour over the cold water. Add the salt and break up with the hands until crumbly. Add the eggs and continue to mix with the hands. Heat the lard and scald the flour with it. The fat should be hot but not smoking. Mix well with a wooden spoon. Stir in the cheese, then cover and place in the refrigerator for a few hours or overnight. Mix in the ½ cup of water. Oil the hands and a baking tray, and roll mixture into balls. Bake in a very hot oven until golden (about 20 minutes or more). Serve while hot, with butter.

Melted lard or rendered fat is essential for this recipe and oil or margarine cannot be substituted.

POTATO ROLL
ROCAMBOLE DE BATATAS

*This potato roll appears in various forms through Latin America and is suitable as an
entrée, luncheon dish or an accompaniment to a main course.*

Serves: 4-6
Cooking time: 30-35 minutes
Oven temperature: 220°C (425°F)

1 kg (2 lb) potatoes
salted water
2 tablespoons butter
½ cup milk
2 egg yolks
salt
pepper
4 tablespoons flour
1 teaspoon baking powder
2 egg whites
1 cup ham, chopped
1 tablespoon parsley, chopped
1 onion, chopped
1 peeled tomato, chopped
½ cup cheese, grated
¼ cup parmesan cheese, grated
tomato and cashew sauce (page 30)

Peel the potatoes, slice and cook in salted water
until soft. Drain, mash and add the butter, milk
and egg yolk. Beat together well, season with
salt and pepper and fold in the flour and
baking powder. Beat the egg whites until stiff
and fold into the mixture. Line a shallow
baking dish with well greased heavy duty foil,
spread the mixture over the foil and bake in a
hot oven until browned (about 20-25 minutes).
Allow to cool for a few minutes before turning
out onto a damp cloth. Peel back the foil and
spread with the combined ham, parsley, onion,
tomato and cheese. Roll up the potato like a
Swiss roll using the cloth to help lift it. Place
the roll into the greased baking dish or
ovenproof platter, sprinkle the parmesan
cheese over and return to a hot oven for 5-10
minutes.

Serve with tomato and cashew sauce.

RE-FRIED BEANS
FRIJOLES RE-FRITOS

Serves: 6
Cooking time: 10 minutes

3 cups cooked kidney beans
½ cup dripping or lard
1 cup onion, chopped
2 cloves garlic, crushed
1 cup peeled tomatoes, chopped
salt
pepper
1 teaspoon dried hot chillis, crushed

Mash the beans roughly with 2 tablespoons of
dripping. Heat the remaining dripping and fry
the onion and garlic for a few minutes. Add the
beans, ½ cup at a time, mashing continuously
with a fork. Continue stirring until all the fat is
absorbed and the beans are almost dry. Add the
tomatoes, salt, pepper and chillis and cook
gently for a few minutes.

Serve re-fried beans as an accompaniment to
grilled meats or as a filling for tacos (page 57)
or enchiladas (page 58).

COCONUT MILK
LEITE DE COCO or LECHE DE COCO

USING FRESH COCONUT
Yield: 1 cup thick milk and 3 cups thin milk
Oven temperature: 220°C (425°F)

1 coconut
¾ cup hot milk
2½ cups hot water

Pierce the eyes at the top of the coconut and drain the liquid into a small jug. (This is *not* coconut milk. It is known as *agua de côco* or coconut water). Place the whole coconut into a hot oven and leave for 10-15 minutes. Carefully remove from oven and, while very hot, strike it sharply with a hammer. As it splits, the meat will fall away from the shell. If you omit the oven heating, you will have to pry the meat from the shell by hand, a long and tiresome job. The brown skin can be quickly removed from the meat with a vegetable peeler. Grate the flesh using a hand grater, a food mill, or blend it in a blender with just enough of the *agua de côco* to moisten it (about 2 tablespoons). Place the grated coconut into a saucepan with the milk and heat, but do not boil. Remove from heat, stand 10 minutes then pour into a sieve. Press the pulp with the back of a spoon to extract as much milk as possible. This is the thick milk. Heat the 2½ cups water with remaining *agua de côco* until boiling and pour through the coconut residue in the sieve. Press with the back of a spoon to extract as much as possible. This is the thin milk.

USING SHREDDED COCONUT

Yield: 1½ cups thick milk and 2 cups thin milk

2 cups desiccated or shredded coconut
2 cups hot milk
2 cups hot water

Place the coconut into a bowl and pour over the hot milk. Stand for 10 minutes, then pour into a fine sieve. Press down with the back of a spoon to extract the thick milk. To extract the thin milk, pour the hot water over the residue in the sieve and press out well.

For the recipes in this book, combine the thick and thin milk and use according to recipe.

Excellent canned coconut milks are available, as is coconut cream in cartons. The cream may be heated in milk or water in the proportions given in a recipe, or the canned milk may be used undiluted. However, recently some sweetened types of coconut milk have been appearing on the market. These may be used for sweet recipes but are not suitable for fish, shellfish or poultry.

RICE WITH COCONUT MILK
ARROZ CON COCO   *BRAZIL, MEXICO*

Serves: 6
Cooking time: 30 minutes

2 tablespoons oil
1 onion, chopped
2 cloves garlic, crushed
2 cups short grain rice
1 cup coconut milk (page 50)
3 cups chicken stock
salt

Heat the oil and sauté the onion and garlic. Wash the rice and add. Cook for a few minutes, but do not brown. Add the coconut milk, the chicken stock and salt to taste. Bring to the boil, cover, and reduce heat to very low. Simmer for about 20 minutes or until all the liquid has been absorbed. Remove from the heat and stand aside with the lid on for 15-30 minutes. The steam in the saucepan will dry and separate the grains. Stir lightly with a fork and serve with fish or prawn dishes.

PIRAO OR ACACA
                                                    BRAZIL

The oil used for pirão *in Brazil is* dende *oil, a crude native palm oil that is bright orange in colour. This is missing in this recipe, but some oil is necessary for texture and consistency.*

Serves: 6
Cooking time: 15-20 minutes

1 cup coconut milk (page 50)
2 cups water
salt
3 tablespoons rice flour
2 tablespoons oil

Blend all the ingredients in a saucepan and stir with a wooden spoon over a gentle heat for about 15 minutes or until the mixture reaches a creamy consistency.

Serve *pirão* with *vatapá* and other Afro-Brazilian dishes. *Pirão* may be cooked until very thick, poured into a greased tin, cut into slices when cold, and placed on a plate beside the *vatapá*.

51

CORN AND HAM CUPCAKES
QUINDINS DE MILHO VERDE E PRESUNTO

The name of these savouries is literally cupcakes, but they are actually little savoury cakes which are perfect to serve with drinks. You may also serve two or three as an entrée with an accompanying sauce. This recipe contains ham, but they are often made with chicken or with prawns.

Yield: 18-20
Cooking time: 20 minutes
Oven temperature: 220°C (425°F)

1 x 500 g (16 oz) can corn kernels, drained
1 onion, grated
salt
¼ teaspoon cayenne pepper
1 cup hot water
5 eggs
250 g (8 oz) ham, chopped
1 tablespoon parsley, chopped
1 tablespoon butter
2 tablespoons parmesan cheese, grated
2 teaspoons rice flour *or* cornflour (cornstarch)

Place the drained corn, onion, salt and cayenne pepper into a saucepan. Cover with hot water, bring to the boil and boil for 5 minutes. Remove from the heat and drain well. Purée half the corn in a blender until smooth and combine with the unblended corn. Place all the corn in a bowl and add the beaten eggs, ham, parsley, butter, cheese and rice flour. Mix very well and check the seasoning. Add more salt if necessary. Grease patty tins well with butter, and fill ¾ full with batter. Stand the patty tins in a pan of water and bake in a hot oven until well browned and firm to the touch. Allow to cool slightly, then loosen edges with a knife and turn out. Serve in paper cases as savouries or as an entrée.

Serve the cupcakes as a first course, surrounded with mashed potato and topped with mushroom or cheese sauce.

VEGETABLE TORTE
TORTA DE LEGUMES

BRAZIL, CHILE AND ARGENTINA

This recipe has become somewhat of a favourite with my family. It is so simple to prepare that it is worthwhile keeping it in mind as an accompaniment to roast meats. However, when cold it is equally good with cold, sliced meats or with barbecues. The recipe is Brazilian but an Argentine friend who also lived in Rio de Janeiro disputes the name, saying that it is obviously a type of tortilla *(omelette).*

Serves: 8
Cooking time: 45 minutes
Oven temperature: 180°C (350°F)

4 eggs
1 cup cooking oil
3 cups plain flour
1 teaspoon baking powder
2 cups diced, cooked potato, carrot and peas
4 spring onions (scallions), chopped
½ cup parsley, chopped
½ cup tomatoes, chopped
pepper
3 chicken stock cubes
2 cups water

Beat eggs lightly, then stir in all the other ingredients. Fold together well and place in a well greased baking dish, 33 x 23 x 8 cm (13 x 9 x 3 in). Bake in a moderate oven for about 45 minutes or until set and golden brown. Remove from oven and cut into triangles to serve. Serve hot or cold.

For an attractive cold plate, bake in a large spring form pan and when cold decorate with overlapping slices of salami, cheese and tomato and garnish with onion rings.

MIDNIGHT CAULIFLOWER
COUVE-FLOR DA MEIA NOITE

BRAZIL

Serves: 6
Cooking time: 30 minutes
Oven temperature: 180°C (350°F)

1 cauliflower
1 cup water
salt
1 onion, grated
2 cloves garlic, crushed
1 tablespoon butter
½ cup oil
1 tablespoon anchovies, chopped
½ cup black olives
1 cup cream
salt
pepper
chopped parsley

Place the cauliflower head down in a large saucepan with the water and salt. Cover and steam until tender (about 10 minutes). Drain and place cauliflower into a greased casserole dish. Combine the other ingredients and pour over the cauliflower. Place in a moderate oven for 30 minutes until browned. Garnish with parsley.

SEASONED PURÉED CORN
HUMITAS   *ARGENTINA*

Humitas, *which is virtually puréed corn with seasonings and cheese, is served in one form or another in every Latin American country. The mixture is frequently wrapped in corn husks and steamed in much the same way that* tamales *are cooked in Mexico. When served this way it is known as* humitas en chala. *I have even seen it steamed in banana leaves.*

Serves: 6
Cooking time: 15 minutes

750 g (1½ lb) corn kernels (fresh or canned)
½ cup milk
1 teaspoon salt
freshly ground black pepper
½ teaspoon ground chillies (optional)
2 tablespoons lard *or* butter
1 onion, chopped
125 g (4 oz) pumpkin *or* squash, finely chopped
1 tablespoon sweet red pepper (capsicum), chopped
¼ cup parmesan cheese, grated

Purée the corn kernels with the milk in a blender (or pass the corn through a food mill then add the milk). Add salt, pepper and chilli. Heat the lard or butter and fry the onion, pumpkin and red pepper for 10 minutes. Add the puréed corn and cook, while stirring, until it thickens a little (about 5 minutes longer). Add the grated cheese, mix well and remove from heat.

Serve in an earthenware dish as an accompaniment to grilled or roasted meats.

TORTILLAS
                                                                   MEXICO

Yield: 12
Cooking time: 2-4 minutes each

2 cups dehydrated masa flour (*masa harina*)
1 teaspoon salt
1 cup warm water

Place the masa flour into a bowl and add the salt. Gradually add the water, mixing constantly. The dough should be firm but soft, and should not stick to your fingers. If necessary, knead gently with your hands and add up to 2 tablespoons of water. Divide the dough into 12 balls and place each one between two sheets of greaseproof paper. Roll with a rolling pin or press with a tortilla press to give rounds of approximately 15 cm (6 in) in diameter. Heat an ungreased frying pan over a moderate heat and cook each tortilla for 1-2 minutes on each side. Wrap in a towel to keep warm while cooking the remainder. They may be kept warm in a low oven for a few hours if necessary, but keep them well wrapped in a towel.

Serve tortillas instead of bread with Mexican meals, or fold or roll with fillings and toppings as suggested on pages 57 and 58.

Roast Beef for Salads (*Carne Assada para Salada*), recipe on page 62, with avocado slices, Stuffed Cucumbers (*Pepinos Rellenos*), recipe on page 43, and Avocado Sauce (*Salsa Guasacaca*), recipe on page 30.

FOLDED SOFT TORTILLAS
TACOS

The taco *is a popular snack or meal made from a* tortilla. *They may be simply a soft* tortilla *folded over a filling of beef or beans, or they may be crisp-fried and then filled. The* tortilla *is often rolled to completely enclose the filling, and then fried in hot oil until crisp. All tacos are served with a selection of toppings such as lettuce, onion, tomatoes, cheese, avocado and sauce. The sauce may be either hot or mild without chillies.*

Serves: 4-6
Cooking time: 10 minutes

12 tortillas (page 54)
1 tablespoon oil
500 g (1 lb) minced (ground) beef
1 onion, chopped
1 clove garlic, crushed
2 tablespoons tomato paste
salt
pepper
2 tablespoons coriander *or* parsley, chopped

Toppings:
1 cup cheese, grated
1 cup lettuce, shredded
1 cup onion, chopped
1 cup tomatoes, chopped

Sauce:
1 cup tomato purée
1 tablespoon onion, grated
½ teaspoon Tabasco sauce
salt
pepper

Make 12 *tortillas* (according to the recipe on page 54) and keep them warm. Heat the oil in a pan and brown the beef, onion and garlic over a medium heat. Add the tomato paste, salt, pepper and coriander, stir and cook for 10 minutes. Remove from the heat. Place about 2 tablespoons of filling onto each tortilla and fold in half. Serve the toppings separately to add according to taste. Combine the sauce ingredients and serve with the *tacos*.

Variation: After adding the filling to the *tacos*, roll up and completely enclose. Fry each *taco* in hot oil, seam-side first, until crisp. Serve with the toppings.

Rolled, Stuffed Beef *(Matambre Arrollado)*, recipe on page 64.

ROLLED FILLED TORTILLAS
ENCHILADAS   *MEXICO*

Serves: 4-6
Cooking time: 30 minutes
Oven temperature: 180°C (350°F)

1 cup tomatoes, peeled
1 clove garlic
2 tablespoons onion, chopped
½ cup green pepper (capsicum), chopped
4 dried hot chillies, crushed (optional)
1 cup stock
salt
pepper
2 tablespoons oil
12 tortillas (page 54)
2 cups cooked chicken, diced
½ cup cheese, grated
½ cup onion, chopped
½ cup lettuce, shredded

Place the tomatoes, garlic, onion, green pepper, chillies and stock into a blender and purée. Add salt and pepper to taste. Pour into a pan and bring to the boil. Simmer for 10 minutes and turn off the heat. Heat the oil in a frying pan. Take one tortilla at a time and dip it into the sauce then fry it quickly in the hot oil for about 1 minute on each side. Drain slightly and lay on a warm plate. When all the tortillas are cooked, place about 2 tablespoons of chicken on each and roll up. Place seam-side down in an ovenproof dish and pour over the remaining sauce. Sprinkle with the cheese and cook in a moderate oven for 20 minutes. Before serving, top with the chopped onion and shredded lettuce.

If preferred, the filling may be pork, beef, cheese or Re-Fried Beans (page 49). Cooked beans often accompany *enchiladas*.

WHEAT TORTILLAS
                                                                MEXICO

Yield: 12
Cooking time: 2-4 minutes each

1 cup plain flour
1 cup wholemeal flour
½ teaspoon baking powder
1 teaspoon salt
2 tablespoons dripping or lard
½ cup water

Sift flours, baking powder and salt into a bowl. Rub in the dripping with your fingertips until distributed through the flour. Add the water and mix to a soft dough, then knead lightly. Divide the dough into 12 balls and roll each one into a round approximately 15 cm (6 in) in diameter. Cook in an ungreased pan over a moderate heat for 1-2 minutes on each side. Wrap in a towel to keep warm.

Beef and Lamb

Beef production is widely distributed throughout Latin America. In many countries the meat is tough, but cooks have devised ingenious and delicious methods of preparing it. The meat is often boiled, shredded and re-cooked with seasonings, and this is the basic method used to prepare the beef fillings used in *tortilla*-type dishes.

The largest producer and consumer of beef in South America is Argentina, and the Argentinians choose the best cuts of meat for *assado* or barbecue. Peru, however, has a shortage of beef because the country has no suitable grazing land, and the climate is unsuitable for most beef breeds. Selling beef and serving it in restaurants is illegal in Peru during the first half of each month.

Throughout Latin America, the drying and salting of beef is a common practice. The meat is painted with a brine solution and dried in the sun, and the result is called *carne seca* or *charqui*. It is an integral part of Brazil's national dish, *feijoada*. (The recipe for this dish is in the Pork, Ham and Veal section because many pork meats are used in its preparation; it is on page 66). The people of north-eastern Brazil live mainly on dried beef, beans, rice and *manioc* meal from the cassava root.

Lamb is raised in Argentina and southern Brazil, where barbecued lamb is very popular. Although it is sometimes available in areas other than the south of Brazil, lamb is often tough with an unpleasant flavour; few Brazilian cooks would choose lamb instead of beef or veal.

In the Andean countries, where some lamb is available, it is often sun-dried in much the same way as beef.

ROAST BEEF
ROSBIFE

This recipe for roast beef is unusual and delicious. Although I generally use rump roast or rib (scotch) fillet, you could use any boneless beef cut. However, the less tender roasts are better when cooked on top of the stove for the whole time instead of transferring to the oven as below.

Serves: 8-10
Cooking time: 1¼-2 hours
Oven temperature: 180°C (350°F)

Marinade:
1 teaspoon salt
2 cloves garlic, crushed
2 large onions, finely chopped
1 small green pepper (capsicum), chopped
freshly ground black pepper
3 tablespoons parsley, chopped
½ teaspoon ground coriander
1 teaspoon dry mustard
juice of 1 lemon
½ cup stout (dark ale)

Other ingredients:
2½ kg (5 lb) rump roast
4 whole cloves
1 tablespoon oil
1 tablespoon butter

Combine all the marinade ingredients. Make four small incisions in the meat and insert the cloves. Pour the marinade over the meat, cover it with plastic wrap and refrigerate overnight. Turn the meat once or twice if possible. Remove the meat from the marinade and wipe dry with paper towels. Place beef in a roasting pan and pour over the oil and melted butter. Place the pan over high heat on top of the stove and brown quickly on all sides. Transfer the roast to a moderate oven and baste frequently with the marinade. Allow 15 minutes per 500 g (1 lb) for rare beef and 30 minutes per 500 g (1 lb) for well-done beef, or use a meat thermometer inserted into the thickest part of the roast to gauge the amount of cooking required. Remove and allow the roast to rest for 15 minutes while you boil and thicken the pan juices.

Serve with corn on the cob, roasted with butter and with jacket baked potatoes. A full-bodied claret is an appropriate accompaniment.

LAMB CASSEROLE
CAZUELA DE CORDERO   *COLOMBIA*

Serves: 6
Cooking time: 1 hour

1 tablespoon butter
2 tablespoons oil
1 kg (2 lb) leg lamb steaks
2 onions, chopped
2 carrots, sliced diagonally
salt
freshly ground black pepper
1 teaspoon sugar
¾ cup strong coffee
½ cup beef stock
1 tablespoon dry vermouth *or* sherry
¼ cup cream

Garnish:
toasted almonds or macadamia nuts

Melt butter and oil in a fireproof casserole and brown the lamb and onions. Pour off any excess fat and add the carrots, salt, pepper and sugar. Simmer 5 minutes. Add the coffee, beef stock and vermouth. Bring to the boil and cook over low heat, uncovered, for 45 minutes to 1 hour or until lamb is tender. Stir frequently, add cream 5 minutes before serving and bring to the boil again. Serve garnished with almonds or macadamia nuts toasted in the oven.

In Colombia or Bolivia this is served with a local black potato. Try it with whole new potatoes, a spinach savoury (page 34) and a full red wine. Don't be put off by the coffee, it really is excellent with the lamb.

PAN ROAST OF LAMB
ASSADO DA PANELA A MODA RIO GRANDE DO SUL   *SOUTHERN BRAZIL*

Serves: 8
Cooking time: 1½ hours

2 kg (4 lb) boned leg of lamb
salt
ground pepper
1 clove garlic, crushed
2 spring onions (scallions), finely chopped
2 tablespoons oil
1 cup hot water
juice of 1 lemon
½ cup dry white wine
1 cup cream

Garnish:
pistachio nuts *or* parsley

Roll the boned leg into a neat shape and secure with string. Season the meat with the salt, pepper, garlic and spring onions. Heat oil and brown the meat on all sides. Add hot water, a little at a time, and continue to cook over medium heat. Pour a little lemon juice over the lamb as it cooks, and add more hot water as it boils away. Cook for 1½ hours. The meat should still be slightly pink in the centre. Remove the meat to a hot platter and cut into thick slices. Add the wine to the pan drippings and bring to the boil. Boil for a few minutes and stir in the cream. Reheat but do not boil, and pour it over the sliced lamb. Serve immediately, garnished with chopped pistachio nuts or parsley.

Serve with whole new potatoes tossed in butter, and halved tomatoes stuffed with cheese, breadcrumbs and basil. A red or white wine is suitable.

61

ROAST BEEF FOR SALADS
CARNE ASSADA PARA SALADA   *BRAZIL*

Serves: 8
Cooking time: 40 minutes-1½ hours

2 onions chopped
2 peeled tomatoes, chopped
1 clove garlic, chopped
2 tablespoons parsley, chopped
1 teaspoon cinnamon
2 tablespoons lemon juice
2 tablespoons oil
1 cup cider vinegar
1 cup dry white wine
1 teaspoon dry mustard
2 kg (4 lb) rump *or* topside roast
1 tablespoon butter
1 x 500 g (16 oz) can beef consommé

Mix the onions, tomatoes, garlic, parsley, cinnamon, lemon juice, oil, vinegar, wine and mustard together. Marinate the beef for 3 hours in refrigerator, turning occasionally. Remove the meat from the marinade. Melt butter in a large heavy pan and brown the drained meat on all sides. Pour over the marinade mixture, cover, and simmer over low heat. Add the consommé gradually during cooking. Allow 10 minutes per 500 g (1 lb) for rare and 20 minutes per 500 g (1 lb) for well done beef. Allow beef to cool in the uncovered pan until cold, then wrap and refrigerate. The pan gravy can be used with steak. Serve sliced with salads.

Many little café bars in Rio de Janeiro serve this delicious meat which is piled onto fresh, French bread rolls. A relish is sometimes served with it, consisting of chopped tomato, onion, parsley, vinegar, sugar, salt and occasionally chilli.

CHILEAN LAMB CASSEROLE
CAZUELA DE CORDERO   *COLOMBIA, CHILE*

Serves: 6
Cooking time: 45 minutes

1 tablespoon oil
1 tablespoon butter
1 kg (2 lb) boneless lamb, cubed
2 onions, sliced
salt
pepper
1 cup beef stock
¼ teaspoon ground cloves
1 piece cinnamon stick
1 teaspoon green ginger, grated
juice of 1 lemon
½ cup cream

Garnish:
roasted almonds
parsley

Heat oil and butter and sauté the lamb and onions until brown. Add salt, pepper, stock, cloves, cinnamon and ginger. Cover and simmer for 30-40 minutes, then add the lemon juice and cook uncovered for 5 minutes longer. Add the cream and reheat. Garnish with roasted almonds and parsley and serve very hot.

Serve with rice and a salad of parsley, mint, onion, tomato, lemon juice, oil and roasted sunflower seeds. This dish needs a full-flavoured red wine.

CREOLE-STYLE STEW
CARBONADA CRIOLLA   *ARGENTINA*

Serves: 6
Cooking time: 45 minutes

½ cup oil
2 cloves garlic, crushed
1 onion, chopped
1 kg (2 lb) round steak
½ cup peeled tomatoes, chopped
¼ cup butter
bunch of mixed herbs
1 small potato, cubed
250 g (8 oz) pumpkin or squash
1 sweet potato
2 cobs of corn, sliced,
   or 1 cup corn kernels
1½ cups beef stock
salt
freshly ground black pepper
¾ cup short grain rice
1 apple, peeled and diced
3 peaches, peeled and sliced
6 dried peaches or pears

Heat the oil in a casserole and sauté the garlic and onion. Add the steak and tomatoes and cook for a few minutes. Add the butter, herbs, cubed potato, pumpkin, sweet potato and corn. Stir with a wooden spoon and add the stock. Season with salt and pepper. Cover with a lid and allow to simmer until cooked but not mushy. Add the rice and cook for 20 minutes longer. Add the apple, peaches and dried fruit and simmer for 5 minutes longer. If necessary, add a little more stock. If there is not enough, the stew will be too thick and heavy.

Variation: This carbonada can be varied by adding 1 cup of pre-soaked split peas or white beans such as haricots. It would be necessary to add a little more stock if these ingredients are used.

This dish is frequently served with a salad of whole, crisp lettuce leaves dressed with oil, lemon and basil. A red burgundy-style wine usually accompanies it.

MEAT FLOWERS
FLORES DE CARNE   *MEXICO*

Serves: 4-6

1 avocado, peeled and seeded
1 cup zucchini, grated
1 tablespoon onion, minced
½ teaspoon ground chillies
2 tablespoons vinegar
2 tablespoons oil
½ teaspoon salt
16 thin slices cold roast beef
thin strips sweet red pepper (capsicum)

Mash the avocado flesh with the grated zucchini and add the onion, chillies, vinegar, oil and salt. Blend together well. Place 1 tablespoonful on each slice of beef. Roll up to resemble a lily leaving one end slightly open. Place a thin strip of red pepper into the open end to resemble a stamen. Arrange on a platter lined with lettuce. If necessary secure each roll with toothpicks.

In Mexico stuffed cucumbers (page 43) are served with this dish.

Serve with onion rings, stuffed cucumbers and crusty sesame rolls or ryebread.

ROLLED, STUFFED BEEF
MATAMBRE ARROLLADO

Serves: 6
Cooking time: 1½ hours

1 kg (2 lb) skirt (flank) steak, flattened
salt
pepper
¼ teaspoon chilli powder *or* paprika
½ cup vinegar
½ cup oil
1 tablespoon parsley, chopped
1 bay leaf

Filling:
250 g (8 oz) spinach, chopped
1 large onion, sliced
3 medium carrots, peeled
2 hard boiled eggs
2 cloves garlic, sliced
salt
pepper
2 tablespoons dried breadcrumbs
stock *or* water to cover

Combine the steak, seasonings, vinegar, oil, parsley and bay leaf. Stand for a few hours or leave overnight in the refrigerator. Drain the beef and lay it out flat. Cover it with a layer of spinach, onion rings, whole carrots and eggs. Add slices of garlic and sprinkle with salt, pepper and breadcrumbs. Roll firmly into a Swiss roll and tie with string. Tuck in the ends. Place into a large pan of boiling stock or water, cover and cook for 1½ hours. Cool the meat roll in the stock. When it is cold, transfer it to a pan. Place a plate on top of the roll and weigh it down with a heavy object for several hours or overnight. Slice and serve.

If preferred, the meat may be rolled in browned crumbs or may be glazed with an aspic when cool.

The *matambré* is usually served cold with a crisp salad and a cottage loaf, but it may be reheated and served with rice. Serve a dry wine with this dish.

Pork, Ham and Veal

These meats are widely used throughout Latin America, whether barbecued, cured or simply roasted. Pork and ham are relatively expensive, though veal is more reasonably priced.

Pork is always lean and is most commonly sold in the form of whole boned loin, known as *lomo* in Spanish-speaking countries and as *lombo* in Brazil. Pork cutlets are also popular, and are often barbecued. Whenever pork is served, regardless of the cooking method, lemon juice is squeezed over the meat as it cooks.

Smoked and cured ham is very popular, as is raw ham. One very common pork cut, known as *pernil*, is virtually fresh ham. It is neither smoked nor cured. It is usually roasted after it has been marinated in wine, lemon juice and herbs. Thinly-sliced raw ham is often included as antipasto; this is a favourite beginning to an Argentine meal.

Pigs' feet are inexpensive, and are traditionally added to the Brazilian national dish, the *feijoada* (page 66). A pig's foot is often added to a pot of simmering beans to enrich the flavour, and it may be included in the making of soup stock.

Veal is widely used throughout Latin America, though not in Peru or in other countries where beef is scarce. South American veal is generally not the milk-fed veal demanded in many European countries, and may therefore be a little tougher.

Pork, ham and veal dishes are normally served as main meals.

COMPLETE BEANS WITH MEATS
FEIJOADA   *BRAZIL*

This is almost the national Brazilian dish. In Rio de Janeiro, at least, Saturday and Sunday are feijoada *days, when it is served at home or in restaurants. It is always served at lunch, as it is a rather heavy meal for evening. The accompaniments given below are also traditional and the* feijoada *would not be complete without them. Unfortunately, the recipe has been adapted considerably because of difficulty in obtaining some ingredients such as sun-dried and salted meats. Red kidney beans have been used because Brazilian black beans are unprocurable in Australia (although available in limited quantities in certain areas of the United States and in London). Dried Oriental black beans (a type of soy bean) are not suitable.*

Serves: 12
Cooking time: 2 hours.

4 cups dried red kidney beans
hot water to cover
1 kg (2 lb) corned (or jerked) beef
500 g (1 lb) round steak, whole
1 smoked pork hock, about 500 g (1 lb)
1 pig's trotter
1 smoked sheep's tongue (optional)
1 tablespoon oil
1 cup onions, chopped
4 cloves garlic, crushed
2 cups peeled tomatoes, chopped
500 g (1 lb) *chorizo* sausages (page 76)
250 g (8 oz) pork speck
1 teaspoon ground black pepper
salt
2 bay leaves
1 cup parsley, chopped
2 spring onions, (scallions), chopped
2 beef stock cubes
extra water as required
Brazilian rice (page 43)
cooked, shredded kale (or spinach)
pepper and lemon sauce (page 30)
peeled, sliced oranges
farofa (page 44), (optional)

Wash the beans, cover them with hot water and soak for 2 hours. Drain and cover with about 3 litres (5 pints) of fresh hot water. Bring to the boil and add the corned beef, round steak, pork hock, pig's trotter and smoked tongue. Cover and simmer for 1 hour. Heat the oil and sauté the onions and garlic, then add the tomatoes and the *chorizos*. Fry over medium heat for a few minutes and add to the beans. Place the speck into the hot pan and brown on all sides. Add it to the beans, together with the pepper, salt, bay leaves, parsley, spring onions and stock cubes. Mix well, cover and cook for an hour longer, adding more water if required. When beans are cooked and meats tender, remove and separate all the meats. Traditionally the tongue is sliced and placed in the centre of a large platter with the other sliced meats arranged around it. The beans are served from a casserole and the other accompaniments served separately. The pepper and lemon sauce is very hot, so may be omitted if you prefer a milder dish.

As well as the accompaniments mentioned, fresh French bread rolls are served and a good *cachaça* (white rum) with lime or lemon juice is the traditional drink.

66

CHICK PEA CASSEROLE
CAZUELA DE GARBANZOS   *MEXICO*

Serves: 6-8
Cooking time: 1½ hours
Oven temperature: 180°C (350°F)

2 cups dried chick peas
hot water to cover
¼ cup oil
1 kg (2 lb) boneless lean pork
2 cloves garlic, crushed
2 onions, chopped
250 g (8 oz) bacon, chopped
2 tablespoons sweet red pepper (capsicum),
    chopped
1 x 500 g (16 oz) can tomato purée
1 tablespoon chilli powder *or* 1 tablespoon
    crushed, dried chillies (less if desired)
2 teaspoons salt
½ cup vinegar
chopped parsley

Wash the chick peas and cover with hot water. Let stand for 1 hour. Drain, cover with fresh hot water and bring to the boil. Cook over low heat for 1 hour then drain. Heat the oil in a flameproof casserole. Cut the pork into 3 cm (1 in) cubes and brown in the oil. Add the garlic, onions, bacon and red pepper and cook for a few minutes. Add the tomato purée, chilli powder, salt and chick peas to the casserole. Mix well and add the vinegar. Cover and bake in a moderate oven for 1½ hours. Garnish with parsley.

Serve with corn chips or fried bread cubes and a green salad.

VEAL WITH OKRA
QUIABADA   *BRAZIL*

Serves: 4
Cooking time: 1 hour

2 tablespoons oil
500 g (1 lb) boneless veal, cubed
1 veal shank bone
1 clove garlic, crushed
2 onions, sliced
salt
pepper
½ cup parsley, chopped
500 g (1 lb) okra, sliced
90 g (3 oz) bacon, chopped
1 tablespoon dried, ground prawns
pumpkin seeds *(pepitas)* for garnish

Heat the oil and sauté the veal and the shank. Add the garlic, onions, salt, pepper and parsley. Cook over moderate heat for a few minutes then add the sliced okra, bacon and dried prawns. Cover the pan and cook over low heat until meat and okra are tender (1 hour). You may need to add some water during cooking as the okra is rather sticky. Serve hot, garnished with shelled roasted pumpkin seeds *(pepitas)*.

This dish is traditionally served with rice and *farofa* (page 44).

Serve with ribbon noodles tossed with butter and sprinkled with paprika and a celery and walnut salad. A light red wine would be a good accompaniment.

AMAZON STYLE PORK
PORCO NA MODA AMAZONAS

Serves: 6
Cooking time: 15-20 minutes

1 kg (2 lb) boneless, lean pork

Marinade:
½ cup dry white wine *or* vermouth
⅓ cup lemon juice
1 clove garlic, crushed
1 teaspoon sugar
salt
pepper
¼ cup oil
1 bay leaf
1 teaspoon chopped rosemary
1½ cups fine breadcrumbs
½ cup ground cashews *or* peanuts
1 teaspoon grated lemon rind
1 cup oil

Sauce:
1 tablespoon oil
1 tablespoon butter
1 large onion, sliced
1 tablespoon mayonnaise
2 tablespoons cream
2 tablespoons coconut milk (page 50)
¼ teaspoon dried dill
¼ teaspoon tarragon
2 spring onions, finely chopped

Combine the wine, lemon juice, garlic, sugar, salt, pepper, ¼ cup oil, bay leaf and rosemary. Add the pork and marinate for at least 30 minutes. Remove the pork and reserve the marinade. Combine the breadcrumbs, nuts and lemon rind. Coat the pork in this mixture. Heat 1 cup oil in a large, shallow pan over a moderate heat. Add the pork and brown, turning frequently to prevent burning. Drain the pork and place it in an earthenware serving dish. Keep hot.

Sauce: Heat 1 tablespoon oil and butter and sauté onion rings till soft but not brown. Pour in the reserved marinade, bring to the boil, lower heat and simmer for 10 minutes. Add the mayonnaise, cream and coconut milk, mix well and add the herbs. Reheat but do not boil. Pour the sauce over the pork in a line down the centre and garnish with the spring onions.

The pork may be prepared and cooked well in advance and reheated in the oven later while you prepare the sauce.

Serve with ribbon noodles, cooked and tossed in browned butter and chopped parsley. A salad of tomato, onion, black olives and palm hearts is a good accompaniment. This dish needs a chilled white wine, not too dry.

CREOLE STEW
LOCRO CRIOLLO

This recipe is one of many types of locros *or stews which are popular in Argentina and Colombia, particularly during the winter months. They are named according to the regional ingredients. Each has a grain base, such as whole wheat, dried beans, dried maize kernels or fresh corn kernels. This recipe is based on dried beans, but the same recipe can be used with another grain or another meat. The vegetables may also vary.*

Serves: 6-8
Cooking time: 1½ hours

2 cups dried beans (haricot, lima or navy)
hot water to cover
salt
250 g (8 oz) boneless, lean pork, cubed
250 g (8 oz) bacon, chopped
500 g (1 lb) boneless veal, cubed
250 g (8 oz) pumpkin, sliced
2 sweet potatoes, sliced
½ cabbage, cut into wedges

Sauce:
2 tablespoons oil
½ cup spring onions (scallions), chopped
2 teaspoons sweet paprika
3 *chorizo* sausages, sliced (page 76)
½ cup water

Soak the beans in water for 2 hours. Drain and place in a large fireproof casserole. Cover with fresh water and add salt. Bring to the boil and add the pork and the bacon. Cook for 1 hour, covered. Remove the lid and add the veal. Continue to cook, stirring occasionally. After 10 minutes add the pumpkin, potatoes and cabbage. Do not stir in the vegetables; they should remain at the top. When the vegetables are cooked, remove them with a slotted spoon and keep warm. Continue to cook the meats and beans, uncovered, until tender and the liquid is reduced. Taste and add more salt if necessary. Heat the oil in a pan and fry the spring onions gently, without browning. Season with the paprika and mix well. Lower the heat and add the *chorizo* slices and a little water. Simmer for 5 minutes. Serve the bean and meat mixture with some of each vegetable in individual bowls and serve the sauce in a separate bowl to add as you wish.

Usually this dish forms the entire main course, accompanied only with French bread. An entrée of salad or potato croquettes often precedes it. A young, light red wine is the usual accompaniment.

LIVER AND HAM CROQUETTES
CROQUETTES DE FIGADO E PRESUNTO   BRAZIL

Serves: 6
Cooking time: 30 minutes
Oven temperature: 180°C (350°F)

250 g (8 oz) liver
1 tablespoon oil
2 cloves garlic, crushed
1 onion, chopped
¼ cup parsley, chopped
salt
pepper
1 cup chicken stock
500 g (1 lb) ham, diced finely
60 g (2 oz) bacon, finely chopped
few drops Tabasco sauce
½ teaspoon ground oregano
½ teaspoon nutmeg
1 tablespoon rice flour *or* cornflour
**   (cornstarch)**
2 tablespoons lemon juice
1 egg
breadcrumbs

Remove membranes from the liver and chop into small pieces. Heat the oil and lightly sauté the liver with the garlic, chopped onions, parsley, salt and pepper. Add the stock and simmer until the liver is cooked and the stock reduced. Purée the liver mixture with the ham in a blender, or chop very finely. Place the bacon into a cold pan and heat slowly over a moderate heat so that the bacon fat is rendered. Add the minced mixture and sauté lightly. Season with Tabasco sauce, oregano and nutmeg. Blend the flour and lemon juice and stir in. Cook for a minute then mix in the egg and blend well to combine. Remove to a bowl, allow to cool, and place in the refrigerator to chill. Form into croquette shapes and roll in the breadcrumbs, pressing them firmly onto the surface. Place in a greased, shallow baking dish and brown in a moderate oven for 30 minutes, turning once.

Serve with chilli sauce, braised lettuce with blue cheese sauce and hot sesame rolls. A cabernet wine is a good accompaniment.

70

LEMON PORK
CERDO CON LIMON

Serves: 6
Cooking time: 30 minutes

1 kg (2 lb) boneless, lean pork
2 tablespoons flour
¼ cup oil
1 tablespoon green ginger, grated
2 onions, sliced
½ cup peeled tomatoes, chopped
2 tablespoons parsley, chopped
½ cup lemon juice
2 cups chicken stock
few drops Tabasco sauce (optional)
2 tablespoons mayonnaise

Garnishes:
lemon wedges
chopped parsley

Cut meat into 3 cm (1 in) cubes and sprinkle with flour. Heat the oil and add the pork and ginger. Cook over medium heat for a few minutes, turning with a wooden spoon. Add onions, tomatoes and parsley, cook for a few minutes more and add the lemon juice, stock and Tabasco sauce. Reduce heat and simmer slowly uncovered until the pork is tender and the stock is reduced. Just before serving, stir in the mayonnaise. Garnish with lemon wedges and chopped parsley.

Throughout Latin America, pork is always served with lemon wedges as a garnish.

It is best not to serve this dish with rice as it draws away from the piquancy of the sauce. Instead, try sliced baked potatoes, and a salad of grated carrots, orange slices and walnuts with a French dressing. A very dry white wine is best with this dish.

RABBIT IN PIQUANT SAUCE
COENJO EN MOLE PICANTE

This recipe is for rabbit but similar spicing is used in many areas of Latin America with pork, veal, kid and even with guinea pig.

Serves: 6-8
Cooking time: 45 minutes

1 2 kg (4 lb) rabbit
salt
pepper
1½ teaspoons ground ginger
2 tablespoons oil
250 g (8 oz) small onions, peeled
1 green apple, peeled
1 clove garlic, crushed
1 teaspoon thyme
2 bay leaves, crushed
½ cup milk
1 cup beef *or* chicken stock
½ teaspoon cayenne pepper (optional)

Clean the rabbit and cut into 6 or 8 serving pieces. Season with salt, pepper and ginger. Heat the oil in a large, heavy pan and cook the rabbit pieces for about 10 minutes until browned. Remove to a plate. Add the onions to the pan and stir over moderately high heat until they are browned. Grate the apple and add to the onions in the pan. Add the garlic, thyme and bay leaves while stirring. Return the rabbit pieces to the pan and pour over the milk and stock. Add cayenne pepper if desired, cover, and simmer over low heat for about 30 minutes or until tender.

Serve with rice, green salad and a fruity white wine.

71

ROAST SUCKLING PIG
LECHON ADOBADO

I sampled this recipe for suckling pig while spending Christmas with some friends at their home in Uranga, outside Rosario in Argentina. They lived alongside the local bakery, so the pig was cooked in the bread oven to crispy, succulent perfection.

Serves: 10
Cooking time: 2½-3 hours
Oven temperature: 220°C (425°F)

salt
pepper
3 kg (6 lb) suckling pig
2 cloves garlic, crushed
½ cup wine vinegar
1 cup oil
1 teaspoon paprika
1 cup parsley, chopped
¼ cup white wine
1 cup lemon juice
coarse salt
oil

Rub the salt and pepper into the pig and place it in a roasting pan. Mix all the ingredients together except the lemon juice, coarse salt and extra oil. Pour over the pork. Marinate for at least 1 hour. Add the lemon juice. Roast the pig in a hot oven for 2 hours. Remove from the oven, place the pork skin side up and rub with coarse salt and oil. Return to the oven, increase the oven temperature to 250°C (475°F) and cook for 30 minutes more.

Serve on a hot platter surrounded by whole baked apples, lemon wedges and roasted whole potatoes. A crisp green salad, dressed with oil and lemon, a fresh crusty French loaf, and a good chablis will complement this meal.

SMOKED PORK WITH FRUIT SAUCE
PORCO DEFUMADO COM MOLHO DE FRUTAS

Serves: 6
Cooking time: 15 minutes

2 tablespoons butter
⅓ cup spring onions (scallions), chopped
1½ tablespoons flour
1 x 500 g (16 oz) can chicken consommé
½ cup dry vermouth
½ teaspoon dry mustard
1 tablespoon fruit chutney
1 tablespoon sultanas
1 tablespoon peanuts, chopped
1 tablespoon lemon juice
12 x 1 cm (½ in) thick smoked pork slices
   or 6 x 1 cm (½ in) thick ham steaks

Garnish:
prunes

Heat butter in a large pan and sauté the onions over medium heat. Stir in flour and gradually add consommé and vermouth. Stir until slightly thickened and add mustard, chutney, sultanas, peanuts and lemon juice. Add the pork slices and simmer for 10-15 minutes. Transfer to a shallow heated serving platter and garnish with prunes.

Serve with spinach savoury (page 34), fresh rolls and a rosé wine.

Skewered Spiced Ox Heart (*Anticuchos*), recipe on page 78.

PORK WITH CITRUS SAUCE

LOMBO COM MOLHO DE GELEIA

Serves: 6
Cooking time: 1 hour

1 kg (2 lb) boneless pork loin
1½ cups milk
2 cloves garlic, crushed
4 allspice berries, crushed
1 teaspoon nutmeg
½ teaspoon paprika
1 teaspoon salt
juice of 1 lemon
1 teaspoon Worcestershire sauce
1 teaspoon mustard
2 tablespoons plain flour
90 g (3 oz) bacon, chopped
½ cup dry white wine
2 cups chicken stock
1 tablespoon lime marmalade
1 tablespoon orange peel, grated

Prepare the meat the day before serving. Cut the pork into 3 cm (1 in) regular cubes, place in a bowl and cover with milk. Cover and place in refrigerator for a few hours. Drain off the milk and dry the meat with kitchen paper towels. Season with the garlic, allspice, nutmeg, paprika, salt and lemon juice. Mix in the Worcestershire sauce and mustard and mix till all the pork is coated. Cover and leave in refrigerator overnight. Remove the pork and dust it lightly with plain flour. Place the bacon into a large heavy-based pan and heat to render some of the fat. Add the pork and cook over medium heat until browned. Pour over the wine and cook until all liquid is evaporated (about ½ hour). Add the stock and cook over low heat, uncovered, for ½ hour. Dissolve the lime marmalade in the sauce, add the orange peel and adjust seasoning if necessary. Return to boil and simmer for a few minutes.

To enhance the flavour of this dish, serve simply with rice and baked apples.

Chicken Cooked in Milk *(Frango no Leite)*, recipe on page 84, and Coconut Soup *(Sopa de Côco)*, with separate garnishes, recipe on page 22.

TANGY SPICED PORK
CERDO PICANTE   *BOLIVIA*

Serves: 4-6
Cooking time: 1¼ hours

2½ cups water
1½ cups split peas
1 onion, chopped
1 large carrot, grated
2 strips lemon peel
1 bay leaf
1 clove garlic, crushed
3 tablespoons green celery leaves, chopped
1 teaspoon salt
1 tablespoon butter
1 teaspoon ground cummin
2 tablespoons oil
1 teaspoon salt
750 g (1½ lb) boneless, lean pork
½ teaspoon cummin
1 teaspoon ground cardamom
½ teaspoon ground chillies

Garnish:
lemon slices
stuffed olives

Place water, split peas, onion, carrot, lemon peel, bay leaf, garlic and celery leaves in heavy-based saucepan and bring to the boil. Reduce the heat, cover and simmer for 1 hour or until the peas are almost puréed. Stir occasionally during this time. Remove bay leaf and stir in the salt, butter and cummin. Place in a greased shallow serving dish and keep warm. Heat oil and salt over high heat. Cut the pork into small cubes and add. Brown very well until crisp and cooked. Add all the remaining spices and stir well to coat. Cook for 5 minutes longer. Arrange the spiced pork over the peas and garnish with slices of lemon and stuffed olives.

Serve with a salad of tomatoes and parsley, topped with crumbled feta cheese and jacket potatoes, and a rosé.

CHORIZO SAUSAGES
CHORIZOS CRIOLLO ESPECIALES   *ARGENTINA*

Although these sausages contain some beef, they are basically pork. This recipe is so delicious that I thought it worth including for those people who can purchase casings from the butcher and fit them on a mincer attachment. Alternatively, if you have an obliging butcher, he might put your mixture into casings for you. Saltpetre is available from butchers or pharmacies. No assado (barbecue) in Argentina is complete without chorizo sausages.

Yield: 20-24 x 10 cm (4 in) sausages

1 kg (2 lb) boneless pork
500 g (1 lb) round steak
250 g (½ lb) fresh bacon, cured and only lightly salted
2 g (½ teaspoon) saltpetre
salt
2 teaspoons oregano
6 peppercorns, crushed
½ teaspoon ground hot chilli
1 cup dry white wine or 1 cup vinegar

Cut all meats into small pieces and place in a bowl with saltpetre, salt, oregano, peppercorns, chilli and wine. Cover and leave in the refrigerator for at least 12 hours. Mince coarsely and pack into sausage casings. Twist into small sausages or into horseshoe shapes. These sausages are at their best when cooked over coals for a barbecue but they may be fried or roasted. Prepare them one or two days in advance if possible.

76

Churrasco: Barbecue

Barbecued meat or *churrasco* has become part of life in southern Brazil and also in Argentina (where it is known as *assado*). Each region has its own method of preparing and cooking the meat, but certain basic requirements are the same everywhere.

The fire, started with kindling wood, is usually made with charcoal. It should be sheltered from the wind, as good, long-lasting coals are necessary. Either dig a slight hollow in the ground or use a few rocks or bricks for protection. The meat is cooked either on a spit over the fire or on long skewers inserted into the ground and angled over the fire.

In the region of Brazil near Rio de Janeiro, the meat is brushed with a brine solution prior to cooking, and brushed again every time it is turned. In the more southerly areas of Brazil and in Argentina, the meat has coarse salt pounded into it with the side of a mallet. If you wish, use the handle of a knife to press the coarse salt into both sides of the meat, as it is important not to break and flatten the fibres too much. If using the brine method, add about 1 tablespoon salt to 1 cup water.

Crushed garlic, oil, lemon, herbs or pepper are often added to the brine; only in the barbecue restaurants or *churrascarias* is a brush used to apply it. At home a bunch of herbs tied together is used to give extra flavour, and a frequent combination is several stalks of parsley with one or two spring onions, a bay leaf and fresh coriander.

By keeping the meat a reasonable distance — 30 cm (12 inches) — from the coals, rapid cooking is prevented, otherwise the meat will be overcooked outside and raw on the inside. The bones are not usually removed for a *churrasco*, but if they are the meat should be left in rather large cuts.

The meat should be beautifully crisp, outside and moist and flavoursome on the inside. To serve, carve the cuts into thick slices.

Beef, pork, lamb or chicken can all be cooked *churrasco* fashion, using your choice of cut. If you have a large number of guests, it may be better to spit roast a whole sucking pig or lamb - all that is needed is more time, as well as more attention to turning the animal every so often. A marinade with garlic, lemon, rosemary and marjoram is suitable for spit roasted lamb. Stuff the body cavity with bunches of fresh herbs such as parsley and mint.

Accompaniments for a *churrasco* can be varied, but the *gauchos* of southern Brazil eat nothing more than toasted *manioc* meal *(farofa)* with it. I have included a wheat *farofa* recipe in the Accompaniments section (page 33), if you wish to try this with your barbecue.

Sausages cooked on skewers also accompany the *churrasco*. The types best suited are *chorizos*, bratwurst, knackwurst and pepperoni.

A bowl of chopped tomato and onion is served, seasoned with vinegar, salt and sugar. The variety of salads served with *churrasco* is very wide, so choose your favourite to go with the meat.

SKEWERED SPICED OX HEART
ANTICUCHOS

These Peruvian delicacies may be bought from street vendors in the big cities such as Lima. They are always cooked over glowing coals, so they are very suitable for a barbecue. You may, of course, cook them under a griller but the flavour is not quite the same. The original anticuchos *are prepared with beef heart, but I have often substituted chicken livers, and kidneys or cubed liver.*

Serves: 6
Cooking time: 10 minutes

1 kg (2 lb) ox heart, cubed

Marinade:
1 cup vinegar
2 cloves garlic, crushed
3 dried, hot chillies, crushed
1 teaspoon cummin seeds, crushed
1 teaspoon salt
ground black pepper
1 tablespoon coriander *or* **1 tablespoon parsley, chopped**

Sauce:
½ teaspoon Tabasco sauce
1 tablespoon tomato paste
1 tablespoon oil
ground black pepper
1 teaspoon hickory smoked salt or liquid smoke *or* **1 teaspoon Worcestershire sauce**

Mix together all the marinade ingredients and pour over the ox heart cubes in a glass or pottery bowl. If the marinade does not completely cover the meat, add more vinegar. Cover and refrigerate overnight. Remove the heart and reserve the marinade. Mix the sauce ingredients and add ¾ cup of reserved marinade. Thread the meat onto bamboo or wooden skewers and brush with the sauce. Cook over hot coals, or under a hot griller for 6-10 minutes, turning frequently and brushing with the sauce.

It is wise to soak the skewers in water for 30 minutes before use. This should prevent them catching fire while grilling.

Serve with a mushroom and onion salad, topped with a sour cream and basil dressing, and a robust red wine.

SPIT-ROASTED SUCKLING PIG

LEITAO ASSADA

Serves: 12-14
Cooking time: 6-8 hours

Marinade:
2 cloves garlic, crushed
2 tablespoons salt
black pepper
3 bay leaves
2 cups dry white wine
1 cup cider vinegar
1 cup lemon juice

Other ingredients:
1 x 7 kg (15 lb) suckling pig
2 large onions studded with 3 cloves each
spray of rosemary
bunch of parsley
oil for basting

Mix the marinade ingredients together and pour over the pig. Stand overnight and turn the pig occasionally to distribute the marinade. Remove the pig and place the onions, rosemary and parsley in the body cavity. Prepare the fire according to the *churrasco* method to ensure very hot coals. If you do not have a metal spit, use a sharpened stake and insert it through the pig so that it is as balanced as possible. Brush the skin with oil and place the pig approximately 30-35 cm (12-14 in) from the coals. Turn frequently and brush with oil. Allow about 8 hours cooking for a pig of this weight. You may have to move the pig aside while you prepare fresh coals if the fire appears to be dying, but do not replace the pig until the flames have died down and only coals remain.

MIXED BARBECUE
(CHURRASCO MISTO)

Serves: 6
Cooking time: 20-30 minutes

500 g (1 lb) rump or fillet steak
250 g (8 oz) lean, boneless pork
6 *chorizo* sausages (page 76)
6 fresh pork (continental) sausages
12 small onions, peeled
1 lemon, cut into wedges
2 tablespoons oil
2 tablespoons vinegar
1 tablespoon chopped parsley
1 teaspoon paprika
1 bay leaf, crushed
salt
freshly ground black pepper

Cut the steak and the pork into 5 cm (2 in) cubes. Thread the meats onto 6 skewers together with the *chorizos*, pork sausages, onions and lemon wedges. Combine the oil, vinegar, parsley, paprika, bay leaf, salt and pepper and brush over the skewered meat. Grill over hot coals about 10-15 minutes each side or until cooked as desired. Brush frequently with the oil and vinegar mixture.

NOTE: Serve with a salad, *farofa* (page 44) and a claret, or light beer.

Poultry

Throughout Latin America, poultry appears regularly on the table. Rich and poor alike enjoy it, and cooks in every country have their own methods of preparing it.

The most common poultry in Mexico is chicken, but turkey is used for more special occasions. A cooked bird is coated with prepared sauce or the poultry is steamed slowly with the sauce in a special clay cooking vessel.

Peruvians create delicious chicken and duck dishes which are combined with rice. This combination, which is common to Chile and Argentina, is a variation of the Spanish *arroz con pollo*.

Poultry of all types is of great importance in Brazilian cooking. Chickens are often cooked over the coals (*na brasa*), and brushed regularly with a marinade flavoured with garlic and coriander. Duck and turkey are also widely used, roasted with unusual stuffings and sauces.

The stew-like soups of Colombia and Bolivia are based on chicken stock. Corn, potatoes and other vegetables are cooked in this. Another favourite way of cooking poultry is to simmer the meat in fruit juices or coconut milk. Nuts, pumpkin seeds or chillies may be added.

BONELESS STUFFED CHICKEN

FRANGO DESSOSSADA COM RECHEIO DE VITELLA   *BRAZIL*

Although this chicken is usually served cold, I have often served it hot with an accompanying sauce. For a cold buffet it is really a very special centrepiece. Boning the chicken is not difficult, but take your time over the first one you attempt.

Serves: 6
Cooking time: 1½ hours
Oven temperature: 180°C (350°F)

1 x 2 kg (4 lb) chicken
500 g (1 lb) ground veal
175 g (6 oz) bacon, chopped
1 x 250 g (8 oz) can unsweetened chestnut purée
    or 250 g (8 oz) sliced mushrooms
2 eggs
¾ cup white breadcrumbs
4 spring onions (scallions), chopped
2 teaspoons ground coriander
1 clove garlic, crushed
salt
freshly ground pepper
1 tablespoon dry vermouth *or* white wine
1 tablespoon butter
almond sauce (page 31)

To bone the chicken: place the chicken on a board, breast side down. Use a sharp, short-bladed knife and slit the skin down the underside. Use the blade and fingers to work the skin with flesh from the carcass. When the leg joint is reached, cut the sinew that joins the thigh to the carcass. Hold the top of the thigh bone and scrape flesh from the bone, then continue on down the drumstick until all flesh is removed. Cut the skin if necessary at end of drumstick to release the bone. Do the same to the other leg. Sever the wing joint from the carcass, though you need not bone the wing. Continue to work down around the carcass until the breastbone is reached. Very carefully work the flesh from the breastbone, releasing the skin over the bone as you go. Take care not to split the skin. Remove the whole carcass.

To prepare the stuffing, mix together all the ingredients except the butter. Stuff the chicken, forcing some stuffing into the leg cavities and allowing some bulk in the breast area. Sew the chicken together with a trussing needle and turn it so that it is seam side down in a baking dish. Tuck the wings underneath, tie the drumsticks together and plump up the breast with your hands. Spread the butter over the skin and bake it in a moderate oven for 1½ hours until golden. Baste occasionally. If serving hot, remove the chicken from the oven and stand for 15 minutes before carving. For cold chicken, remove from the oven and compress under a plate with a weight on top for 1 hour. Cool the chicken then wrap it and refrigerate. (The chicken is much easier to carve when cold.)

If serving the chicken hot, accompany with almond sauce, parsleyed potatoes and a green salad. A selection of salads should accompany cold chicken, and garlic bread is delicious with either hot or cold chicken.

QUICK CHICKEN CORNMEAL MOULD
CUSCUZ RAPIDO DE FRANGO   *BRAZIL*

Cornmeal in various forms is used extensively throughout Latin America. Many different meats and vegetables are combined with it and this recipe varies according to what is available. There are many different types of cuscuz made in Brazil, using chicken, prawns, fish or ham. All of them, however, require lengthy preparation and careful steaming in a special vessel resembling a colander. Fortunately, I managed to locate a recipe which eleminates this and which is suitable for local cornmeal.

Serves: 4-6
Cooking time: 25 minutes

2 cups oil
2 onions, grated
1 x 500 g (16 oz) can spaghetti sauce
salt
pepper
3 chicken stock cubes
1 bay leaf
1 x 500 g can (16 oz) can palm hearts, sliced
1 cup peas, cooked
1 tablespoon green pepper (capsicum), chopped
1½ cups cooked chicken meat, coarsely chopped
¼ cup parsley, chopped
2 spring onions (scallions), chopped
2 cups cornmeal *(polenta)*

Garnishes:
hard boiled egg, sliced
black olives
tomato slices
sardines or shelled prawns
strips of sweet red pepper

Heat oil and sauté the onions, then add the sauce, salt, pepper, stock cubes and bay leaf. Cook for several minutes, then add the sliced palm hearts and the liquid from the can, the peas, green pepper and chicken, chopped parsley and spring onions. Add the cornmeal and stir the mixture with a wooden spoon over moderate heat. Cook for 15 minutes. Grease a medium-sized mould, pudding basin or mixing bowl. Decorate the greased mould or basin with sliced egg, olives, tomato slices, red pepper and sardines or prawns. Arrange in an attractive design on the base and around the side of the mould or basin. Carefully add the cornmeal mixture (which should be thick) to the basin without disturbing the decoration. When all the mixture is used, press down well to compact the cornmeal. Stand aside for a minute, then unmould onto a serving platter. Cut into wedges to serve. If any decoration remains in the bowl, simply press it back into place.

Cuscuz makes a delicious and simple lunch dish served with a salad. It also may be served cold and is perfect for a picnic or barbecue.

CHICKEN COOKED IN MILK
FRANGO NO LEITE *BRAZIL*

I first tasted this dish when travelling north from Rio de Janeiro and found it both unusual and delicious. It is not difficult to prepare, but it does need a little care.

Serves: 6
Cooking time: 1½ hours

Marinade:
1 chicken stock cube
2 cloves garlic, crushed
1 teaspoon salt
1 tablespoon lemon juice
1 tablespoon vinegar
freshly ground black pepper

Other ingredients:
1 x 2 kg (4 lb) chicken
2 tablespoons oil
1 large onion, sliced
2 tablespoons parsley, chopped
1 tablespoon tomato paste
½ teaspoon ground coriander
5 cups milk (at room temperature)
½ cup shredded spring onions (scallions)

Combine the marinade ingredients and pour over the chicken. Cover the chicken with a plastic wrap and refrigerate overnight, turning it once or twice if possible. Drain the chicken. Heat the oil and brown the chicken on all sides. Remove the chicken and set aside. Fry the onion and parsley in the oil and stir in the tomato paste and coriander together with the reserved marinade. Pour in the milk and heat slowly. The milk should curdle and when it does, replace the chicken in the pan. Cover closely and cook over a moderate heat until chicken is tender (about 1 hour). Remove the chicken to a plate. Leave the saucepan uncovered and boil rapidly until the liquid has evaporated. Continue to cook over moderate heat until the curds begin to brown. Use a metal spoon to scrape the pan to prevent sticking. Return the chicken again and brown with the curds. Transfer to a hot platter and garnish with finely shredded spring onions.

Serve with potato cakes (grated potato, salt, egg and flour fried in oil), green salad and a chablis-type wine.

CHICKEN WITH PUMPKIN SEEDS
XIN-XIN

This recipe is an Afro-Brazilian dish that originated with the Negro slaves who prepared ritual dishes for the gods as part of their Umbanda *(black magic) religion.*

Serves: 4
Cooking time: 45 minutes

1 x 1.5 kg (3 lb) chicken
3 cups water
¼ cup dried, ground prawns
1½ teaspoons salt
¼ cup oil
½ cup parsley, chopped
2 onions, sliced
½ teaspoon dried chillies
   or few drops Tabasco sauce
60 g (2 oz) shelled pumpkin seeds (*pepitas*)
2 teaspoons ground coriander
¼ cup oil
rice cooked with coconut milk (page 50)

Garnishes:
parsley
whole pumpkin seeds

Cut the chicken into serving pieces and place in a large pan with the water, ground prawns, salt, ¼ cup oil, parsley, onions and chillies. Cover and steam until the chicken is tender (about 30 minutes). Remove the lid and cook until the liquid is well reduced. Set aside 6 whole pumpkin seeds for garnish. If the green pumpkin seeds are roasted, grind the remainder in a blender or food mill. If they are not roasted when you buy them, place them in a heavy saucepan with a lid and place over medium heat for a few minutes until they pop, then grind them in a blender. Add the ground pumpkin seeds to the chicken, together with the coriander and oil. Reheat and serve garnished with parsley or whole pumpkin seeds.

Serve with rice cooked with coconut milk and lightly cooked, sliced carrots and zucchini seasoned with nutmeg and butter. A fruity white wine complements this meal.

MEXICAN TURKEY
MOLE POBLANO DE GUAJOLOTE

MEXICO

The sauce that gives this recipe its name is possibly the most famous from Mexico, and is used to accompany chicken and even pork dishes. The ingredients tend to vary according to regional availability. Reduce the amount of chilli if you prefer a milder sauce. The turkey is usually cooked whole, but is easier to handle if cut into pieces.

Serves: 8-10
Cooking time: 1 hour 40 minutes

1 x 4 kg (8 lb) turkey
water to cover turkey
½ cup oil
2 teaspoons dried, hot chillies
  or **1 tablespoon chilli powder**
3 cloves garlic
2 large onions
2 green peppers (capsicums)
2 slices toast
½ cup almonds
2 cups peeled tomatoes, chopped
2 tablespoons toasted sesame seeds
1 teaspoon cinnamon
2 teaspoons ground coriander
4 cloves
salt
pepper
30 g (1 oz) unsweetened cooking chocolate

Place the turkey in a large saucepan and cover with salted water. Simmer for 1 hour. Remove turkey and reserve 2½ cups of the stock. Heat the oil in a pan and brown the turkey well, then transfer it to a large casserole or baking dish. If using dried chillies, cover with boiling water for 5 minutes. Place the soaked chillies or chilli powder, garlic, onion, peppers, toast, almonds, tomatoes, 1½ tablespoons sesame seeds and spices into a blender. Blend to a smooth purée or pass through a food mill if no blender is available. Heat a little oil in a pan and cook the sauce for about 5 minutes. Add the stock and the chocolate and stir with a wooden spoon until the chocolate melts. Pour the sauce over the turkey so that it is well coated and simmer, covered, over low heat for 40 minutes. Garnish with the remaining seeds.

Serve with whole new potatoes, corn, and a salad of lettuce, sliced avocado and onion. A dry champagne goes well with this dish.

86

ROAST DUCK
PATO ASSADO

Serves: 6
Cooking time: 1 hour
Oven temperature: 180°C (350°F)

1 x 2 kg (4 lb) duck
½ cup orange juice
salt
freshly ground pepper
strip of lemon peel
1 onion, chopped
1 spring onion (scallion), chopped
1 clove garlic, crushed
½ cup dry white wine
¼ teaspoon ground chillies (optional)
1 tablespoon oil
2 tablespoons rosella *or* cranberry jelly
2 tablespoons raisins
white grapes (optional)
baked oranges (page 41)

Split the duck in half and place in a shallow glass bowl. Mix together the orange juice, salt, pepper, lemon peel, onion, spring onion, garlic, wine and chillies. Pour over the duck and marinate for 1-3 hours, turning occasionally. Remove duck and place in a roasting pan. Brush with the oil and bake in a moderate oven for 1 hour. During this time brush the duck with the reserved marinade mixed with the jelly. When the duck is cooked, transfer to a heated platter. Add the raisins to the pan drippings, together with any remaining marinade. Bring to the boil on top of the stove and cook for a few minutes, scraping the bottom of the pan as the duck cooks. If you do not have enough liquid, add stock or water. Pour the sauce around the duck and garnish with a few white grapes if desired.

Serve with steamed potatoes, baked oranges and red or rosé wine.

TURKEY CASSEROLE
CAZUELA DE PAVO

Serves: 8
Cooking time: 1½ hours
Oven temperature: 180°C (350°F)

1 x 3.5 kg (7 lb) turkey

Marinade:
1 clove garlic, crushed
2 teaspoons salt
freshly ground black pepper
1 cup orange juice
2 cups dry vermouth

Other ingredients:
2 tablespoons butter
2 tablespoons oil
500 g (1 lb) small onions, peeled
2 cups peeled tomatoes, chopped
1 bay leaf
½ cup toasted almonds, ground
1 cup stuffed olives, sliced

Garnish:
ham, finely chopped

Cut the turkey into serving pieces and place in a large, shallow dish. Mix together the garlic, salt, pepper, orange juice and vermouth and pour over the turkey. Cover and refrigerate overnight. Remove turkey and reserve the marinade. Heat butter and oil in a heavy casserole and brown the turkey pieces. Add the onions and brown slightly then add the tomatoes, bay leaf and marinade. Cover the casserole and bake in a moderate oven for 1 hour. Remove cover, stir the nuts into the sauce and add the olives. Place in the oven, uncovered, for another 30 minutes. Adjust seasoning if necessary. Garnish with very finely chopped ham.

Serve with foil roasted potatoes topped with sour cream, corn on the cob and a light dry white wine.

CHICKEN IN CORNMEAL BATTER
(POLLO REBOZADO)   *BOLIVIA*

Serves: 4-6
Cooking time: 45 minutes

2 tablespoons cornmeal *(polenta)*
½ teaspoon salt
freshly ground black pepper
¾ cup milk
2 eggs
1 x 2 kg (4 lb) chicken
½ cup oil
2 onions, sliced
3 cups fresh or canned peeled tomatoes,
  chopped
2 tablespoons chopped parsley
½ cup dry white wine
½ teaspoon ground coriander
½ teaspoon oregano
salt
pepper

To make the batter place the cornmeal, salt and pepper in a bowl, add the milk and lightly beaten eggs and beat well. Cut the chicken into serving pieces and dry them with kitchen paper towels. Heat half the oil in a large pan. Dip the chicken pieces into the batter and fry in the hot oil until well browned. Remove chicken and drain on absorbent paper. Heat the remaining oil in a flameproof casserole and sauté the onions for a few minutes. Add the tomatoes and parsley and cook for a few minutes longer. Add the wine, coriander, oregano, salt and pepper and bring to the boil. Add the chicken pieces to the sauce, cover and simmer over low heat for 30 minutes or until chicken is cooked.

NOTE: Serve with boiled potatoes and a crisp green salad. A light lager-style beer is usually served in Bolivia, but a dry white wine may be served instead.

MARINATED STEAMED CHICKEN
(POLLO PIBIL)   *MEXICO*

Serves: 4-6
Cooking time: 1 hour

1½ cups orange juice
½ cup lemon juice
1 onion, finely chopped
1 clove garlic, crushed
¼ teaspoon ground cloves
½ teaspoon cinnamon
1 teaspoon salt
freshly ground black pepper
1 teaspoon ground cumin
1 teaspoon liquid annatto (optional)
1 x 2 kg (4 lb) chicken, cut into 6 pieces
2 tablespoons oil
tortillas (pages 54-58)

To make the marinade place orange juice, lemon juice, onion, garlic, cloves, cinnamon, salt, pepper, cumin and annatto in a shallow dish. Add the chicken pieces to the marinade and turn to coat them on all sides. Marinate for several hours or overnight in the refrigerator. Remove chicken pieces from marinade and reserve the marinade. Heat the oil in a flameproof casserole and brown the chicken quickly on all sides. Pour over the reserved marinade and bring to the boil. Cover and simmer over low heat for 1 hour or until tender. Serve with tortillas.

For yucatan-style chicken, wrap each piece of marinated chicken in banana leaves and steam in a metal colander for 1 hour.

NOTE: Fresh *tortillas* and steamed rice are the usual accompaniments. A moselle-style white wine complements the flavour of the dish.

Seafood

The fish markets along Latin America's huge coastline sell everything from tiny fresh sardines to huge gropers. The fishmonger will dress the fish as required — whole cleaned, cut into steaks or filleted, or, in the case of sardines, with head and backbone removed. Several kinds of prawns are also offered, with crabs, lobsters, mussels, oysters, clams, scallops, baby squid, octopus and sometimes eels.

Much of the seafood offered for sale has been caught only hours before, and all prawns, crabs and shellfish are sold 'green' or uncooked. Everything is fresh; frozen fish of any kind is most unusual.

However, sometimes seafood is dried, and dried salt cod is very popular throughout Latin America. After freshening in cold water, the cod is cooked according to the chosen recipe. It is stronger in flavour than fresh fish.

Some of the most appealing seafood feasts are prepared by groups of young boys who gather shellfish from the rocks or from sandy seabeds. The shellfish are placed in a large drum with a little salt water, a thick layer of newspaper is placed on top, and the drum is placed over a fire until the shellfish steam and the shells open. When the newspaper is removed, there is an aroma of freshly steamed shellfish, sharpening the appetite for the feast.

FISH BALLS WITH GINGER
BOLINHOS DE PEIXE COM GINGEMBRE   *BRAZIL*

Serves: 6
Cooking time: 25 minutes

1 tablespoon capers
1 x 45 g (1½ oz) can anchovy fillets
3 white bread rolls
½ cup hot chicken stock
500 g (1 lb) fish fillets
4 medium onions, quartered
4 tablespoons plain flour
⅔ cup cream
2 eggs
cayenne pepper to taste
1 teaspoon ground nutmeg
2 litres (8 cups) chicken stock
1 tablespoon butter
3 cups milk
salt
white pepper
1 tablespoon green root ginger, grated
2 cups white breadcrumbs
1 tablespoon lemon juice

Garnish:
parsley

Pound capers and anchovy fillets to a paste in a mortar and pestle. Break the bread rolls into pieces and pour ½ cup very hot chicken stock over them. Leave to soak for a short time. Mince the fish fillets, soaked bread rolls, anchovy paste and onions finely in a mincer, food processor or blender. Place the fish mixture in a bowl and add the flour, cream, eggs, cayenne pepper and nutmeg. Mix well and roll the mixture into small balls. Bring the 2 litres (8 cups) of stock to the boil. Add salt if necessary. (If using stock cubes you should not need more salt.) Drop the fish balls into the boiling stock, cover the saucepan and turn off the heat immediately. Allow to stand for 15 minutes and the fish will be cooked. Remove the balls and allow them to drain well. Place them in a casserole and keep warm. Melt butter in a saucepan and add the milk, salt and pepper. Add the ginger root and breadcrumbs and beat with a rotary beater. When the sauce is smooth, remove from the heat and stir in the lemon juice. Pour the sauce over the fish balls and serve immediately. Garnish with parsley.

Serve with boiled potatoes which have been tossed in browned butter, and with fresh peas topped with fried onions and bacon. The dish is usually accompanied with light beer, but I prefer a dry white wine.

90

Opposite: Fish Balls with Ginger *(Bolinhos de Peixe com Gingembrê)*, recipe on this page.
Overleaf: Shellfish with Garlic Crumbs *(Accorda de Mariscos)*, recipe on ·page 98.

FISH MOULD WITH PRAWN SAUCE
PUDIM DE PEIXE COM MOLHO DE CAMARAO   *BRAZIL*

Serves: 6
Cooking time: 1 hour
Oven temperature: 180°C (350°F)

500 g (1 lb) white fish fillets
salt
pepper
500 g (1 lb) potatoes, cooked and mashed
1 tablespoon potato flour *or* cornflour
  (cornstarch)
1 cup milk
1 tablespoon cream
2 eggs, separated

Sauce:
250 g (8 oz) prawns
1 tablespoon butter
1 tablespoon flour
1 cup fish stock *or* chicken stock
1 cup cream
salt
pepper

Cut the fish into finger lengths, season with salt and pepper and set aside. Combine the mashed potatoes, potato flour or cornflour, milk, cream and egg yolks. Beat the egg whites until stiff and fold into the potato mixture. Grease a 6-cup mould and place a layer of fish in the base followed by a layer of potato mixture. Continue until the mould is filled, finishing with a potato layer. Stand the mould in a pan of water and bake in a moderate oven for 1 hour.

Sauce: Shell and devein the prawns. Melt the butter and blend in the flour. Cook for a minute and stir in the stock. Cook until thickened, stirring constantly. Add the prawns and cream, stir to mix, reheat and season with salt and pepper. Unmould the fish and cover with the sauce.

Serve with cheese scones, halved, topped with butter and sesame seeds and grilled. A crisp green salad and a dry white wine also go well with this dish.

Opposite: Angels' Double Chins *(Papas De Anjo)*, recipe on page 104.
Previous page: Seafood Stew *(Vatapa)*, recipe on page 96.

SEAFOOD STEW
VATAPA

Vatapá is a traditional dish brought by the African slaves when they were put to work on the old sugar plantations in Bahia in the north of Brazil. Some of the ingredients are unavailable here, such as dendê *oil — a crude palm oil which is not assimilated by the body and which adds only an orange colour and a certain texture. I have therefore adapted this recipe to suit our conditions. I have made this version many times, and it is almost indistinguishable from the original.*

Serves : 6-8
Cooking time: 1¼ hours

1 kg (2 lb) fish fillets, cut into fingers
500 g (1 lb) cooked prawns, shelled and deveined
salt
freshly ground black pepper
squeeze lemon juice
1 cup oil
2 cloves garlic, crushed
3 onions, chopped
2 cups tomatoes, peeled and chopped
2 teaspoons ground coriander
2 bay leaves
1 cup parsley, chopped
2 spring onions (scallions), chopped
4 cups coconut milk (page 50) *or* 1 250 g (8 oz) carton creamed coconut in 4 cups milk
250 g (8 oz) roasted cashews
60 g (2 oz) roasted peanuts
2 cups white breadcrumbs
pirão (page 51)
pepper and lemon sauce (page 30)

Season the fish and prawns with salt and pepper and sprinkle with lemon juice. Heat the oil and fry the garlic and onion over a medium heat for 5 minutes. Add the tomatoes, coriander, bay leaves, parsley and spring onions and stir with a wooden spoon. Pour in 2 cups of the coconut milk or dissolved creamed coconut, cover the pan and simmer for 30 minutes. Lay the fish pieces on top, cover again and steam for 10 minutes. Remove the fish carefully with a slotted spoon and set aside. Put the cashews, peanuts and breadcrumbs in a blender or food mill and process until finely ground. Stir into the *vatapá* with the remainder of the coconut milk. Stir over a low heat until the mixture boils and becomes thick and creamy. Add the prawns and fish and reheat gently. If the mixture becomes too thick, add a little extra milk

Vatapá is traditionally accompanied with *pirão* and with pepper and lemon sauce. The latter gives this dish its hot and spicy flavour.

LOBSTER BAKED IN PINEAPPLE
LAGOSTIM GRATINADO NO ABACAXI   *BRAZIL*

Serves: 4-6
Cooking time: 10 minutes
Oven temperature: 220°C (425°F)

1 large ripe pineapple
1 tablespoon butter
2 cloves garlic, crushed
2 large onions, grated
1½ cups tomatoes, peeled and chopped
½ cup mushrooms, sliced
1 teaspoon mustard
¼ cup Marsala wine
2 spring onions (scallions), sliced
2 tablespoons parsley, chopped
750 g (1½ lb) lobster meat, cooked
1 cup white sauce
salt
pepper

Garnish:
1 tomato
hard boiled egg
stuffed olives
radish roses
celery curls

Cut the pineapple in half lengthwise, right through the crown. Leave a shell of 4 cm (1½ in) and remove the remainder of the pineapple flesh, cut it into cubes and place it in a colander to drain. Melt the butter and add the garlic, onion, tomatoes, mushrooms and mustard. Stir and cook for a few minutes. Add the wine, spring onions and parsley and cook for 5 minutes. Stir in the lobster, white sauce and pineapple cubes. Fold together well and allow to cool slightly. Dry the pineapple shells and fill with the mixture. Place in a hot oven for 10 minutes to brown. Remove to a serving platter. Cut a tomato into wedges and place upturned on the pineapple to form petals of a flower. Centre the tomato flowers with a slice of boiled egg and an olive slice. Garnish the platter with radish roses, celery curls and the lobster legs.

This dish may be served as a main course or in smaller servings as an entrée. A full, white burgundy is a good accompaniment.

PAN COOKED OYSTERS   *BRAZIL*
OSTRAS DA PANELA

Serves: 4
Cooking time: 5 minutes

¼ cup butter
1 tablespoon Worcestershire sauce
1 tablespoon lemon juice
¼ teaspoon cayenne pepper
2 tablespoons green celery leaves, chopped
pepper
2 dozen shelled oysters
1 cup cream
1 x 500 g (16 oz) can palm hearts, drained
¼ cup butter
crisp cooked bacon pieces

Heat ¼ cup butter and add the Worcestershire sauce, lemon juice, cayenne, celery leaves, salt and pepper. Add the oysters and their juice and bring to the boil. Simmer over a low heat for 2 minutes. Add the cream and reheat but do not allow to boil. Place sliced palm hearts in the bottom of each bowl and spoon the oysters and sauce over the top. Top each with a knob of the remaining butter and sprinkle with crisp pieces of bacon.

Serve crusty bread, a green salad and either dry champagne or a white burgundy

SHELLFISH WITH GARLIC CRUMBS
ACORDA DE MARISCOS
BRAZIL

As some of the cookery styles of Brazil came from the early Portuguese settlers, some recipes are similar to those of Portugal. This one has been slightly changed to suit the Brazilian taste.

Serves: 4
Cooking time: 35 minutes
Oven temperature: 180°C (350°F)

6 cloves garlic, crushed
¾ cup oil
4 cups soft breadcrumbs
500 g (1 lb) cooked shellfish (crab meat and shelled prawns)
⅓ cup fresh coriander *or* ⅔ cup parsley
⅓ cup chopped parsley
salt
freshly ground pepper
4 eggs
lemon wedges

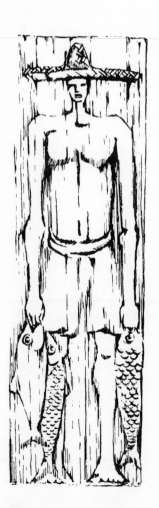

Heat the garlic and oil in a large shallow casserole in a moderate oven until the garlic is golden. Mix in the crumbs. Bake for 25 minutes, stirring occasionally, until crumbs are crisp and golden. Spread shellfish over the top with coriander, parsley, salt and pepper. Take immediately to the table, break eggs over the top and stir lightly with a fork to mix. Serve immediately, as the heat of the crumbs cooks the eggs. Serve with lemon wedges.

The *açordá* can be made in individual casseroles for each guest. Give each person a sherry glass containing 1 tablespoon of port wine and an egg yolk. Everyone then stirs the port and egg into their sizzling crumbs.

Accompany with a salad of orange slices, cucumber slices and green olives. A chilled fruity white wine is excellent.

PRAWNS WITH SESAME AND PUMPKIN SEED SAUCE
PIPIAN DE CAMARONES   *MEXICO*

One of the ingredients which makes this Mexican dish unique is pepitas or pumpkin seeds. They are readily available at health food stores and delicatessens, but make sure you buy the shelled ones, which are green and elongated.

Serves: 4-6
Cooking time: 25 minutes

1 kg (2 lb) uncooked (green) prawns
1 cup water
3 tablespoons oil
2 tablespoons sesame seeds
2 cloves garlic, crushed
3 tablespoons pumpkin seeds (*pepitas*)
1 onion, chopped
1 teaspoon dried hot chillies, crushed
1 teaspoon ground coriander
¼ cup parsley
2 tablespoons lemon juice
salt

Shell and devein prawns, leaving the last tail section intact, and set aside. Place the prawn shells and water into a pan, cover and simmer for 15 minutes. Pass the stock through a fine sieve and reserve. Place the oil, sesame seed, garlic, *pepitas* and onion into a pan. Stir over a medium heat until the seeds begin to brown. Remove from heat and add the chillies, coriander and parsley. Pass through a blender or food mill and add the prawn stock. Return sauce to the pan and stir constantly over low heat until it is bubbling. Add the prawns and cook gently for 10 minutes, then stir in the lemon juice. Add salt to taste.

Serve very hot, garnished with lemon slices and accompanied with boiled rice.

PRAWNS AND SHELLFISH WITH RICE
CAMARONES Y MARISCOS CON ARROZ   *MEXICO*

Serves: 6
Cooking time: 40 minutes

2 tablespoons butter
1 onion, chopped
2 cups long grain rice
½ teaspoon saffron
½ teaspoon paprika
4 cups hot water
2 chicken stock cubes
1 teaspoon salt
750 g (1½ lb) cooked prawns, shelled
250 g (8 oz) scallops
½ cup parsley, chopped
¼ cup fresh fennel, chopped
   or 1 teaspoon dried fennel

Heat the butter in a large heavy pan and add the onion and rice. Cook until they begin to brown, and add the saffron, paprika, water, stock cubes and salt. Cook over low heat for about 20 minutes or until the rice is almost cooked. Add the deveined prawns and the scallops. If the scallops are very large they should be sliced or chopped. Stir the seafood lightly into the rice and cook for 5 minutes longer. Add the parsley and the fennel and continue to cook over low heat until the water is absorbed and the rice is dry. Remove from heat, cover with a tightly fitting lid and let stand for 10 minutes

In some regions, hot chilli is used instead of paprika, and extra prawns, crabmeat or mussels are used in place of the scallops.

99

COD IN PASTRY
EMPANADA GALLEGA

This dish of fish encased in pastry is traditionally prepared with salt cod, but if this is difficult to obtain, smoked cod may be substituted. If you are able to buy salt cod, soak it overnight, changing the water several times, and boil it in fresh water until cooked.

Serves: 6
Cooking time: 50 minutes
Oven temperature: 180°C (350°F)

Pastry:
4 cups plain flour
2 teaspoons baking powder
1 teaspoon salt
½ cup butter
2 eggs, beaten
⅓ cup water

Filling
½ cup oil
500 g (1 lb) onions, chopped
1 sweet red pepper, chopped
½ cup peeled tomatoes, chopped
500 g (1 lb) cooked cod, flaked

Pastry: Place dry ingredients in a bowl and cut in the butter with the back of a fork. Add the lightly beaten eggs and water, and add a little more water if necessary to give a soft dough. When well combined, place on a floured board and knead lightly. Roll out to a large circle and place filling on one half. Moisten the edges with water and fold over. Press edges together with a fork. Brush over with milk or beaten egg and bake in a moderate oven for 50 minutes.

Filling: Heat oil and fry onions lightly. Add red pepper and tomatoes and cook for 1 minute. Add fish and season to taste. When cold, use as filling for pastry.

NOTE: Serve *empanada* with a cucumber, onion and tomato salad for a complete meal. A dry rosé goes well with it.

SEAFOOD WITH GREENS
EFO

This recipe traditionally contains the crude native palm oil, dendê. *As this is not generally available, I have used cooking oil for texture and tomato paste for colour.*

Serves: 4-6
Cooking time: 20 minutes

500 g (1 lb) cooked prawns, shelled
2 tablespoons dried prawns (optional)
1 clove garlic
2 onions, peeled
½ teaspoon dried hot chillies
1 teaspoon coriander
375 g (12 oz) spinach *or* kale, shredded
500 g (1 lb) white fish
2 tablespoons oil
1 tablespoon tomato paste
¼ cup oil
salt
pepper
lemon wedges

Place the cooked prawns, dried prawns, garlic, onions, chillies and coriander into a blender and purée or pass through a food mill. Wash spinach or kale, shake dry and cook in a covered saucepan with the water clinging to the leaves. When cooked, drain off the liquid, and add the spinach or kale to the prawn mixture. Cut the fish into small pieces and remove the skin and bones. Heat 2 tablespoons oil in a pan and fry the fish until browned and cooked. Add the fish to the prawn and spinach mixture. Stir in the tomato paste, oil, salt and pepper. Reheat and serve garnished with lemon wedges.

Serve with rice or *pirão* (page 51). Carrots steamed with a little chicken stock, butter and nutmeg are also delicious. A chilled, fruity rosé goes well with this dish.

BAKED FISH WITH OLIVE SAUCE

PESCADO CON ACEITUNAS

Serves: 6-8
Cooking time: 40 minutes
Oven temperature: 200°C (400°F)

1 x 2 kg (4 lb) snapper
salt
pepper
1 tablespoon lemon juice
2 firm bananas
2 tablespoons butter
2 tablespoons oil
¼ cup spring onions (scallions), chopped
2 tablespoons sweet red pepper (capsicum), chopped
½ cup stuffed olives, sliced
1 teaspoon grated lemon peel
¼ cup dry white wine
2 tablespoons parsley, chopped
salt
pepper

Garnish:
lettuce, shredded

Rub the fish with salt, pepper and lemon juice and place the peeled bananas in the body cavity. Spread the butter in a large baking dish and lay the fish on it. Heat the oil and sauté the spring onions, red pepper and olives for a few minutes. Add the lemon peel, wine, parsley, salt and pepper and cook for 5 minutes. Pour the sauce over the fish and bake in a moderately hot oven for 40 minutes. Baste once or twice with the sauce during this time. When the fish is cooked, place carefully on a serving platter, remove bananas and spoon the olive sauce over it. Garnish with finely shredded lettuce and the sliced bananas.

The fish is usually served with rice and crusty bread. A very dry white wine is a suitable accompaniment.

Desserts

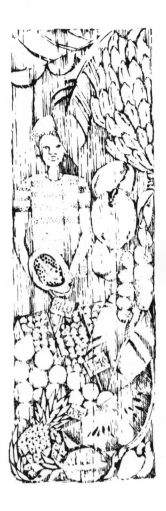

After a normal family meal, dessert in Latin America often consists of a home-made fruit sweet served with a wedge of fresh cheese. This dessert is made by boiling fruit and sugar together; when the mixture is very thick it is turned out to form a loaf, which can be sliced. The most popular dessert served with cheese is the milk sweet known as *dulce de leche* (*doce de leite* in Brazil). I have given two methods of preparation in this section (page 115).

Latin American sweets are sometimes made with fruits or vegetables, which are not used in this way elsewhere. An example is the versatile avocado used for soups, main courses, and in this case ice cream (page 107).

Fresh fruit is often served after a meal, and the South American cook is generally most discerning about quality. Baked desserts using milk, eggs and rice are served both to family and to guests.

The biscuits and little cakes in this section are often served with tea or coffee. In restaurants throughout Latin America, the customer is encouraged to try small amounts of several dessert items and to sample several little cakes and biscuits.

The more exotic desserts, particularly those needing many eggs and those with rich syrups, are reserved for festive occasions or when entertaining guests. The *papas de anjo* (page 104) are usually made in individual serving sizes in restaurants and cake and pastry shops. For larger groups of people or during festive dinners, the dessert is often a large *papão* decorated with glazed fresh fruit. It comes to the table dripping with rich rum or liqueur syrup, and is a highlight of the festive occasion.

ANGELS' DOUBLE CHINS

PAPAS DE ANJO *BRAZIL*

This delightful Brazilian sweet may be made in two forms. I usually put the mixture into a tube mould and pour the syrup over it in the mould. The mixture can also be placed in patty cake tins and the little cakes removed and dropped into the syrup. As it is a very rich sweet, it should be served in small amounts only.

Serves: 10
Cooking time: 15 minutes (small papas*)*
or 40 minutes (large papão*)*

2 egg whites
10 egg yolks
1 tablespoon plain flour
1 teaspoon baking powder

Syrup:
2 cups sugar
1½ cups water
1 vanilla bean *or* 1 teaspoon vanilla essence
1 tablespoon port *or* rum

Beat egg whites until stiff and frothy. Continue beating and add the egg yolks, one at a time. Beat at high speed for about 15 minutes or until double in volume. Add the flour and baking powder and fold in lightly with a rubber spatula. Grease patty tins or grease and flour a round tube mould. Pour the mixture into the pans, allowing room at the top for the mixture to rise. It is not necessary to stand the large mould in a pan of water, but I suggest the patty pans be placed in a pan with a small amount of warm water to prevent burning. Bake the small *papas* in a moderate oven for about fifteen minutes; bake the larger *papao* in a slightly hotter oven for about 40 minutes. The *papas* are cooked when browned and a knife inserted in the centre of the *papas* comes out clean.

To make the syrup, dissolve the sugar in the water over gentle heat. Add the vanilla bean (if using vanilla essence add it later), increase the heat and boil steadily until the mixture reaches the thread stage — 110°C (230°F) on a candy thermometer. Remove from the heat and add the port or rum (and vanilla essence if it is used). For a large sweet, make perforations with a toothpick and pour the hot syrup over it in the pan. Use all the syrup, even if the sweet takes a little while to absorb it all. When cold, loosen the edges of the sweet and turn it out. For patty cakes, loosen the edges carefully, turn out, and drop them carefully into the hot syrup. Allow to cool, and serve in compote dishes

I usually serve this dessert with whole strawberries or apricots cooked in orange juice, and offer whipped cream separately.

NUT ICE CREAM
SORVETE DE NOZES   *BRAZIL*

Ice cream is quite easy to make and very suitable for summer entertaining.

Serves: 8

1 x 440 g (14 oz) can condensed milk
3 cups milk
2 tablespoons powdered drinking chocolate
1 tablespoon cornflour (cornstarch)
1 teaspoon vanilla essence
1 cup chopped or ground toasted cashews,
  almonds *or* hazelnuts (filberts)

Garnish:
shaved chocolate *or* whole nuts

Place the condensed milk, 2 cups of milk and the drinking chocolate into a heavy-based saucepan. Place over a low heat, bring to the boil and remove from the heat. Mix the cornflour and vanilla in the remaining cup of milk and add gradually to the saucepan. Return to the heat and stir with a wooden spoon until thickened. Add the nuts, all at once, and boil for a minute. Allow to cool. Pour into a freezer tray and place in the freezer. When the mixture is almost frozen, remove it from the tray and beat well. Return to the freezer. Repeat once more, then freeze completely. Serve in dessert glasses and top with shaved chocolate or whole nuts.

BAKED CARAMEL 'CHEESE'
QUEIJAO   *LATIN AMERICA*

Serves: 6-8
Cooking time: 30-40 minutes
Oven temperature: 180°C (350°F)

1 x 440 g (14 oz) can condensed milk
2 egg yolks
3 egg whites
1 teaspoon vanilla essence

Place the unopened can of condensed milk in a large pan, cover with water and boil for 1 hour. Cool the condensed milk, pour into a bowl and mix in the egg yolks. Beat well with a wooden spoon. Beat the egg whites until stiff and foamy and fold into the other mixture with the vanilla. Pour into a greased mould or basin. Stand the mould in a pan of water and bake in a moderate oven for 30 minutes. Insert skewer into the centre, and if it comes out clean the sweet is cooked.

This is usually served cold with a wedge of cheese.

PRUNE ICE CREAM
SORVETE DE AMEIXAS

Serves: 8

1 x 440 g (14 oz) can condensed milk
3 cups milk
1 teaspoon vanilla essence
3 egg yolks
1 tablespoon cornflour (cornstarch)
1 cup stoned prunes, chopped
2 egg whites

Garnish:
chocolate *or* crushed toffee

Place condensed milk, 2½ cups milk and vanilla in heavy-based saucepan over low heat. Stir with wooden spoon until boiling and add the egg yolks and cornflour mixed with the remaining milk. Mix rapidly, add the prunes and continue stirring until it thickens slightly. Remove mixture and allow to cool. Beat the whites until stiff and fold rapidly into the prune mixture. Pour into freezer trays and when partly frozen, remove and beat well. Return to freezer and repeat beating once more. Return and allow to freeze thoroughly.

Serve in glasses topped with chocolate or crushed toffee.

ROYAL EGGS
HUEVOS REALES

Serves: 6
Cooking time: 20 minutes
Oven temperature: 160°C (325°F)

¼ cup sweet sherry
2 tablespoons raisins
12 egg yolks
1 cup water
1½ cups sugar
1 piece cinnamon stick
2 tablespoons pine kernels *or* almonds

Pour the sherry over raisins and set aside. Beat the egg yolks until smooth and very light in colour. Pour into a greased shallow pan. Stand in another pan of water and bake in a moderately slow oven for 20 minutes until set. When cool, cut the eggs into cubes of about 4 cm (1½ in). Place the water, sugar and cinnamon in a saucepan and dissolve the sugar over very low heat. Increase the heat and boil for 10 minutes. Remove from the heat and transfer the egg cubes carefully to the pan of syrup. When the cubes are well soaked with syrup, transfer them to a serving dish. Stir the raisins and sherry into the syrup and pour over the egg cubes. Sprinkle with the pine kernels or almonds.

COCONUT MOUSSE
MOUSSE DE COCO

Serves: 6

1 x 440 g (14 oz) can condensed milk
1½ cups shredded coconut
1 tablespoon gelatine
2 tablespoons boiling water
3 egg whites

Garnish:
crushed toffee *or* grated chocolate

Place the condensed milk, coconut and gelatine dissolved in the boiling water into a blender. Mix until smooth, pour into a bowl. Beat the egg whites until stiff and fold in. Place in serving dishes and refrigerate for 3 hours or until set. Decorate with crushed toffee or grated chocolate.

AVOCADO ICE CREAM
SORVETE DE ABACATE

Serves: 6

3 large ripe avocados
1½ cups milk
1 tablespoon lemon juice *or* 1 teaspoon lemon
   juice with 1 tablespoon port wine
½ cup sugar
1 cup cream

Peel and seed avocado and purée with milk in a blender or sieve. Add lemon juice and/or port wine, sugar and cream, beat rapidly and pour into a freezer tray. When beginning to freeze, remove and beat well with a fork. Return to freezer and repeat twice more when beginning to freeze again.

Serve in dessert glasses topped with preserved crystallised lemon peel.

WINE CREAM
CREAM DE VINO

Serves: 6-8

1½ cups fresh cream
4 egg yolks
½ cup sugar
1 cup sweet dessert wine

Mix cream, egg yolks and sugar in a double saucepan. Beat with a whisk or rotary beater until a light thick cream is obtained. Remove from heat and add the wine. Combine well, and pour into glass sweet dishes.

PAWPAW FLAN MOULD
FLA DE MAMAO   BRAZIL

Serves: 6

3 cups ripe pawpaw (papaya), peeled
1 x 440 g (14 oz) can condensed milk
½ cup sweet sherry *or* ½ cup orange juice

Place all ingredients into a blender and blend for 3 minutes, or beat all ingredients in the small bowl of an electric mixer at high speed. Pour into moulds and let stand for at least 1¾ hours at room temperature. Turn the flans out of their moulds and they will retain their shape. Once the flans are set and unmoulded, they may be refrigerated if you wish to serve them chilled.

Decorate with glazed orange peel and mint leaves, and serve with cream.

CARAMEL FILLED BISCUITS
ALFAJORES CORDOBESAS   ARGENTINA

These little sweets are quite delicious. They are joined with dulce de leche *(page 115) and topped with sugar glaze (page 115). It is also common in some areas of Argentina to join them with quince jam instead of caramel.*

Yield: 3 dozen
Cooking time: 10 minutes
Oven temperature: 220°C (425°F)

2½ cups flour
1½ teaspoons baking powder
2 teaspoons sugar
pinch salt
grated rind ½ lemon
½ cup butter
2 egg yolks
1 tablespoon milk
dulce de leche (page 115)
⅓ quantity sugar glaze (page 115)

Place flour, baking powder, sugar and salt in a bowl. Add butter and mix in with back of fork. Drop egg yolks and milk into a well in the centre. Use fork to combine then knead lightly and stand 15 minutes. Roll out to 2-3 mm (⅛ in) thickness and cut circles of 6 cm (2½ in) diameter. Prick well with fork and place on greased baking sheet. Bake in hot oven for 8-10 minutes. When cold, join with *dulce de leche* then top with the sugar glaze.

PUMPKIN CANDY
DOCES DE ABOBORA   *BRAZIL*

St John's Day, 24 June, is a very festive day in Brazil. Parties are held on every evening during the week in which the day occurs. Traditional food and drinks are served and characteristically the food contains pumpkin, coconut or corn. These little sweets may be served after dinner with coffee.

Yield: 4-5 dozen
Cooking time: 1 hour

1 cup pumpkin, cooked and mashed
1 cup sugar
3 cups shredded coconut
½ teaspoon cinnamon
2 tablespoons water

Place all ingredients into a heavy saucepan and stir constantly with a wooden spoon over low heat. When the mixture is thick enough to hold its shape (medium ball stage 115°C, or 238-245°F) remove from heat. Turn onto a greased plate and cool overnight. Form into balls and roll in caster sugar. Let dry out in a warm place, either in the sun or in a warm oven with the door open.

LITTLE CHEESE CAKES
QUEIJADINHA   *LATIN AMERICA*

Yield: 25
Cooking time: 30 minutes
Oven temperature: 200°C (425°F)

1 cup shredded coconut
1 x 440 g (14 oz) can condensed milk
1 tablespoon parmesan cheese, grated
2 egg yolks

Mix all ingredients well together and place into patty papers in a patty cake tin. Stand the tin in a larger pan of water and bake in a hot oven for 30 minutes.

These rich little cakes are delicious after dinner instead of the usual dessert.

RICH RICE DESSERT
ARROZ DULCE CON LECHE   *MEXICO*

Serves: 6
Cooking time: 40 minutes

1 cup short grain rice
5 cups cold water
1 x 440 (14 oz) can condensed milk
1 piece cinnamon stick

Place the rice and water into a large saucepan and heat until boiling. Lower the heat and cook, uncovered, until the water is absorbed. Add the condensed milk and cinnamon and mix with a wooden spoon. Cook over low heat for about 10 minutes longer. Pour into a serving dish and sprinkle with extra cinnamon or nutmeg if desired.

Serve plain or with stewed prunes or apricots.

COCONUT BARS
BARRITAS DE COCO   *LATIN AMERICA*

Yield: 5 dozen
Cooking time: 30 minutes
Oven temperature: 180°C (350°F)

1 x 500 g (1 lb) loaf sliced white bread
1 x 440 g (14 oz) can condensed milk
¾ cup milk
shredded coconut

Remove crusts from the bread and cut each slice into 3 fingers. Combine the milk and condensed milk. Dip the bread into the milk and then roll in the coconut. Arrange on a greased baking sheet and place in a moderate oven until browned.

BRAZILIANS
BRASILEIRAS   *BRAZIL*

These little biscuits are very popular in Brazil. I find that the results are better using shredded coconut than using desiccated coconut. Of course, freshly grated coconut is infinitely superior to both.

Yield: 36
Cooking time: 15 minutes
Oven temperature: 180°C (350°F)

1 cup sugar
¾ cup water
1½ cups shredded coconut
1 tablespoon butter
3 tablespoons plain flour
3 egg yolks
vanilla essence

Dissolve the sugar in the water over gentle heat. Increase the heat and boil steadily until the mixture reaches the thread stage (110°C or 230-234°F). Add the rest of the ingredients except the vanilla essence and continue to cook over low heat. Stir constantly with a wooden spoon until the mixture does not stick to the sides of the pan. Allow to cool and flavour with vanilla. Drop small balls of mixture onto greased baking trays and bake in a moderate oven for 10-15 minutes or until golden.

Pawpaw Flan Mould *(Fla de Mamao)*, recipe on page 108.

COCONUT SWEET
COCADA DE COLHER BRAZIL

This sweet can be made in various consistencies. It can be cooked until very firm, cut into slices and served with a wedge of cheese; or like this recipe, it can be softer and may be used as a filling for pastry or served as it is as a dessert.

Serves: 8
Cooking time: 40 minutes

2 cups sugar
1½ cups water
1 clove
1 piece cinnamon stick, *or* 1 teaspoon ground
   cinnamon
6 egg yolks
1 x 440 g (14 oz) can condensed milk
4 cups shredded coconut
1 teaspoon vanilla essence

Place the sugar, water, clove and cinnamon in a saucepan and heat gently until the sugar has dissolved. Increase the heat and boil steadily until you have a thick syrup. Pour half the syrup into a bowl and cool. Remove the cinnamon stick. Beat the egg yolks very well and then beat them into the cooled syrup. Add this mixture to the syrup in the saucepan and continue mixing over a low heat. Add the condensed milk and the coconut. Continue to stir the mixture over a low heat for about 10 minutes or until well combined and thickened. Flavour with vanilla essence and pour into a glass dish.

CARAMELISED BANANAS
BANANADA · BRAZIL

Serves: 6
Cooking time: 1-1½ hours

6 very ripe bananas
1½ cups brown sugar
1½ teaspoons ground ginger, cinnamon *or*
   ground cloves

Peel and mash the bananas or purée in a blender. Measure the pulp and put into a heavy-based saucepan. Add the sugar and spice of your choice. Cook the mixture over a very low heat, stirring constantly with a wooden spoon. Continue cooking until it reaches a deep caramel colour. (The longer the mixture cooks the darker it becomes as the sugar caramelises.) Allow it to cool and shape into a loaf. When cold cut into slices and serve.

This popular Brazilian sweet is traditionally cooked in an earthenware pot. As with all fruit sweets prepared this way, *bananada* is always served with a soft cream cheese. If fresh whey-type cheese that accompanies this dessert is unavailable substitute a wedge of Munster or a similar cheese. If you prefer, serve this dessert with cream and walnuts.

Baked Caramel 'Cheese' *(Queijao),* recipe on page 105.

LITTLE COCONUT KISSES
BEIJINHOS DE COCO   *BRAZIL*

These little biscuits are very popular in Brazil. I find that the results are better using shredded coconut than using desiccated coconut. Of course, freshly grated coconut is infinitely superior to both.

Yield: 36
Cooking time: 30-40 minutes

1 x 440 g can (14 oz) can condensed milk
1½ cups shredded coconut
2 egg yolks
1 tablespoon butter
1 teaspoon vanilla
sugar
cloves or glacé cherries

Put all ingredients into a heavy-based saucepan over low heat. Mix continuously with a wooden spoon until the mixture leaves the sides of the saucepan. Turn out the mixture onto a greased plate and allow to cool. When cold, roll into small balls and cover with sugar. Top each one with a clove or piece of glacé cherry.

SWEET POTATO GLACE
MARROM GLACE DE BATATA-DOCE   *BRAZIL, ARGENTINA, MEXICO*

This dessert is traditionally served with a wedge of soft cream cheese, though it goes very well with compôte of fruit, such as cherries or plums.

Serves: 10
Cooking time: 1-1½ hours

2 cups sugar
2 cups water
1 kg (2 lb) sweet potato, cooked and mashed
1 teaspoon vanilla essence
¼ cup kirsch *or* other fruit liqueur

Heat the sugar and water together over low heat until sugar is dissolved. Increase the heat and boil steadily until the syrup becomes fairly thick. Add the cooked, mashed sweet potato, vanilla and liqueur. Mix continuously with a wooden spoon until the mixture springs back from the sides of the pan. Pour into a cake pan and allow to cool.

MILK SWEET
DULCE DE LECHE

The recipes for dulce de leche *and sugar glaze (also on this page) are required to make fillings and toppings for several Argentinian, Chilean and Mexican sweets. The caramel is used to fill biscuits, cakes and pastries and it is also served by itself as a dessert. The sugar glaze is used instead of icing on many sweets.*

LONG METHOD

Yield: 1½ cups
Cooking time: 2-2½ hours

1 cup sugar
2 cups milk

Put the sugar and milk into a heavy-based pan and place over a low heat until the sugar begins to dissolve. Increase the heat slightly and continue to cook until it begins to thicken and is smooth. (This could take up to 1½ hours.) Continue to cook over a medium heat, stirring with a wooden spoon until the mixture is very thick and caramelised. The mixture should release from the sides of the pan. Turn into a bowl and cool.

QUICK METHOD

Yield: 1½ cups
Cooking time: 1½ hours

1 x 440 g (14 oz) can condensed milk

Place the can of condensed milk, unopened, into a large pan. Cover completely with water and bring to the boil. Cover and cook for 1½ hours, then drain and cool by covering the can with cold water. Turn the caramelised contents into a bowl and use as directed.

SUGAR GLAZE
BANO DE AZUCAR

Yield: 2-3 cups
4 cups sugar
⅓ cup hot water
1 teaspoon lemon juice

Place all the ingredients into a small mixing bowl and beat at high speed until a dry foam is obtained.

FRIED BATTER TWISTS
CHURROS   *MEXICO*

The batter for churros *is traditionally forced through a pastry tube or biscuit forcer into the hot oil. However, the batter may be dropped into the oil with a teaspoon.*

Yield: 3 dozen
Cooking time: 5-8 minutes

3 cups plain flour
2 teaspoons baking powder
1 teaspoon salt
3 cups water
1 tablespoon lemon juice
oil for frying
sugar and cinnamon

Place flour, baking powder and salt into a bowl and mix well. Heat water in a large saucepan and when boiling, add flour, baking powder and salt. Beat well with a wooden spoon until smooth, and mix in the lemon juice. Heat the oil for deep-frying to 190°C (370°F). Force the batter through a pastry or biscuit tube into the hot oil. When golden brown (5-8 minutes), remove and drain on absorbent paper. Roll in sugar and cinnamon and break into 8 cm (3 in) pieces.

COCONUT DESSERT CAKE
BOLO DE COCO   *LATIN AMERICA*

Cooking time: 1 hour
Oven temperature: 180°C (350°F)

3 egg whites
1 cup sugar
1½ cups shredded coconut
¼ cup chopped walnuts *or* almonds
1 teaspoon vanilla essence
¾ cup plain flour, sifted

Garnishes:
cream
strawberries

Beat egg whites till stiff and frothy. Add sugar gradually and continue beating mixture till glossy. Add the coconut and chopped nuts. Flavour with vanilla essence and combine well. Gently fold in the sifted flour. Line the base of a large spring form pan with a circle of heavy duty foil and grease the pan and the foil very well. Place the coconut mixture in the pan and cover with foil. Bake in moderate oven for 30 minutes. Remove the foil and bake for 30 minutes longer, or till golden and cooked. Cool, cut into wedges and serve with cream and strawberries.

ALMOND SNOW
(NIEVE DE ALMENDRAS)

Serves: 6
Cooking time: 1 hour

½ cup sugar
125 g (4 oz) ground almonds
2½ cups milk
4 egg whites
1 tablespoon sherry or orange liqueur

Place sugar, ground almonds and milk in a saucepan and heat to boiling point. Remove from heat and allow to cool. Beat the egg whites until stiff and fold into the milk, using a spatula. Add the sherry or liqueur and mix lightly. Pour the mixture into a well greased pudding basin, or the top of a double boiler. Cover the basin and cook over hot water in a saucepan until firm (about 1 hour). Do not allow the basin to touch the water in the saucepan. Cool, then chill in the refrigerator. Unmould onto a serving plate.

AVOCADO CREAM
CREME DE ABACATE

Serves: 4

2 ripe avocados
1 tablespoon lemon juice
½ cup sugar
½ cup milk
½ cup cream
1 tablespoon port wine *or* sweet sherry

Peel and seed avocados and place in a blender. Pour over the lemon juice, sugar and remaining ingredients. Blend for a few seconds and pour into sweets glasses. Place a slice of lemon on each glass.

PAWPAW (PAPAYA) CREAM
CREME DE MAMAO

Make this dessert only 15-30 minutes before you serve it, as it will set if left to stand too long.

Serves: 8

1 x 750 g (1½ lb) ripe pawpaw (papaya)
¾ cup sugar
1 cup cream
2 tablespoons rum or port wine
glacé orange peel

Peel and remove seeds from the pawpaw. Place the pulp into a blender with all the other ingredients. Blend for a few seconds until combined. Pour into sweets glasses and chill for 15-30 minutes. Serve with glacé orange peel.

MANDARIN OR ORANGE SWEET
MANJAR DE TANGERINA OU LARANJA

These manjar *desserts are made with various fruit juices and are popular throughout Latin America. Any fresh or canned juice may be used such as grape* (uva), *pineapple* (abacaxi), *apricot* (damasco) *or passionfruit* (maracuja), *which is especially popular in Brazil.*

Serves: 6
Cooking time: 15 minutes

1 tablespoon gelatine
½ cup cold water
1½ cups water
1 piece lemon peel
4 tablespoons cornflour (cornstarch)
2 cups mandarin juice *or* 2 cups orange juice
¾ cup sugar

Garnish:
fresh orange slices
cream

Soften the gelatine in ½ cup cold water, then place over hot water until dissolved. Place the remaining 1½ cups water in a saucepan and bring to the boil with the lemon peel. Add the gelatine, mixing with a wooden spoon as you do. Blend the cornflour with the mandarin or orange juice and stir into the saucepan. Add the sugar and continue stirring until the mixture is smooth and thick (about 10-15 minutes). Remove from the heat and discard the lemon peel. Rinse a mould with cold water and pour in mixture. Refrigerate until set and take out of mould just before serving. Garnish with slices of fresh orange and serve with cream.

MANGO PUDDING
PUDIM DE MANGA

Serves: 6
Cooking time: 40 minutes
Oven temperature: 180°C (350°F)

3 or 4 ripe mangoes
1 tablespoon orange juice
½ cup sugar
2 tablespoons cornflour (cornstarch)
3 eggs, separated
orange sauce (*molho de geleia de laranja*)
  (page 31)

Peel mangoes, cut them into pieces and scrape flesh from the seeds. Add the orange juice and sugar then mash very well or use a blender if preferred. Beat in the cornflour and the egg yolks and fold in the stiffly beaten egg whites. Place into a greased mould or pudding basin, stand in a pan of water and bake for 40 minutes in a moderate oven. When cool, unmould and serve with orange sauce.

SAGO WITH PINEAPPLE
SAGU COM ABACAXI   *BRAZIL*

Serves: 6
Cooking time: 25-30 minutes

1 cup sago
4 cups water
2 cups crushed pineapple, fresh or canned
2 cloves
1 cup sugar (optional)
cream for serving
crystallised ginger

Soak the sago overnight in 4 cups of water. Place the sago and water into a saucepan and add the pineapple and cloves. Place over a low heat and stir with a wooden spoon for about 10 minutes or until the sago begins to cook and becomes transparent (if using fresh pineapple you will need to add sugar.) Add the sugar to the hot sago and stir for about 15-20 minutes or until the sago is completely transparent and gelatinous. Pour into a serving dish and allow to cool. Refrigerate until ready to serve. Top with fresh, whipped cream and crystallised ginger.

PORT WINE AND CARAMEL CAKE
TORTA ARGENTINA   *ARGENTINA*

Cooking time: 30 minutes
Oven temperature: 180°C (350°F)

4 eggs
⅔ cup sugar
peel of 1 lemon, grated
2 cups plain flour
2 teaspoons baking powder
¼ cup port wine
1½ cups *dulce de leche* (page 115)
full quantity sugar glaze (page 115)

Separate eggs, beat yolks with sugar until light-coloured, and add lemon peel. Gradually add flour and baking powder. Add the beaten whites to mixture and fold in smoothly with a wooden spoon, until ingredients are just combined. Prepare a round, deep cake tin by greasing with butter, and sprinkle with flour. Place cake in moderate oven for 30 minutes. When cold cut into several layers, sprinkle each with port wine, then spread with *dulce de leche*. Re-form the torte and top with sugar glaze. For special occasions decorate with marzipan or glacé fruit.

RAW APPLE DESSERT CAKE
BOLO DE MACA CRUA PARA SORBREMESA   *BRAZIL*

Cooking time: 1½ hours
Oven temperature: 160°C (325°F)

1 cup oil (not olive oil)
2 cups sugar
2 eggs
3 cups plain flour
1 teaspoon bicarbonate of soda
½ teaspoon salt
1 teaspoon cinnamon
2 teaspoons vanilla essence
3 cups apples, peeled and diced

Combine cooking oil and sugar, add eggs and mix with wooden spoon. Add plain flour, bicarbonate of soda, salt and cinnamon, mix well and stir in vanilla and apple. Combine then place in a greased large loaf pan with a foil base or in a greased spring form pan. Bake in a moderately slow oven for 1½ hours. If you prefer a soft crust, remove, cool, then turn out. For a crisp crust, simply turn off oven and allow to cool.

Serve with fresh cream.

This cake may tend to fall in the centre because the raw apple cooks and collapses.

FROSTED DUMPLINGS
(ROSQUETES)   *ARGENTINA*

Yield: 30-40
Cooking time: 10-15 minutes

500 g (1 lb) plain flour
1 teaspoon bicarbonate of soda
6 egg yolks
½ cup butter or margarine, softened
½ teaspoon anise seeds
½ cup anise liqueur or rum
sugar glaze *(Baño de Azucar)* **(page 115)**

Sift the flour and bicarbonate into a bowl. Add the egg yolks, softened butter and the anise seeds. Mix well until the mixture is smooth. Add the liqueur or rum and blend well. If the dough is too stiff, add a little milk until the mixture is soft but still holds together. Put the dough aside for 10 minutes.

Bring a large saucepan of water to the boil. Break small pieces off the dough and roll gently in the hands to form balls about the size of a walnut. Drop them into the boiling water and cook until they all rise to the surface (about 10-15 minutes). Remove the *rosquetes* to a colander and place in the sun to dry well. When completely dry, cover each one with sugar glaze.

Beverages

Pure fruit drinks are delightful and refreshing features of many Latin American shops. Particularly in Brazil, the shops where they are sold have spectacular displays of fruit of all sorts hanging from the ceiling, draped on strings down the walls and grouped in baskets and boxes on counters.

The *sucos* (juices) of these fruits are prepared by placing them in a blender with sugar and crushed ice; some varieties are strained to remove seeds or skin, but others are simply poured into a glass. The drinks prepared with fruit, milk and sugar are called *vitaminas*; avocado is commonly prepared this way, and once you try it prepared like this you will understand the Brazilian obsession with it. Banana and milk are usually combined with a spoonful of sugar and fine cereal flakes rather like a fine untoasted muesli.

Sucos may also be made by combining fruits. Commonly available are oranges, apples, pawpaws (papayas), pears, plums, peaches, black and white grapes, custard apples, pineapples, mangoes, passionfruit, guavas, rockmelons (cantaloupes), watermelons, persimmons and limes.

The exotic native fruits of Latin America attract the attention of visitors. The *jaboticaba* resembles a purple plum or overgrown black cherry, and has a strange and delicious flavour. The *caju* is a strange little fruit, varying in colour from red to yellow with a little hook at the top; this hook is the fleshy covering of the cashew nut, for *caju* in Portuguese means 'cashew'. It is very popular with the Brazilians, though not to my taste.

Fruit juices may be served before, during and after a meal, as thirst quenchers on a hot day and even as desserts. They may be sipped at any time of the day.

Here are a few of the typical Latin American drinks, most made from fruit or fruit juices. Some are alcoholic, while others are simply refreshing fruit drinks. This section also contains other popular beverages that do not contain fruit.

121

AVOCADO MILK DRINK
VITAMINA DE ABACATE

Serves: 4

BRAZIL

1 large ripe avocado
3 cups cold milk
2 tablespoons sugar *or* sugar to taste

Peel and seed the avocado and place the flesh in a blender or other electric mixer. Add the milk and sugar and mix at high speed for a few seconds until smooth and foamy. Pour into glasses and serve very cold.

BANANA AND MUESLI DRINK
VITAMINA DE BANANA COM AVEIA

Serves: 4

BRAZIL

3 or 4 ripe bananas, peeled
3 cups cold milk
1 tablespoon sugar
2 tablespoons fine muesli *or* wheat germ

Place all ingredients into a blender or electric mixer bowl. Mix at high speed until smooth and thick. Serve cold.

TEQUILA WITH LIME AND ORANGE LIQUEUR
MARGARITA

Serves: 2

MEXICO

1 wedge lime or lemon
coarse salt
60 ml (2 oz) tequila
⅓ cup lime *or* lemon juice
30 ml (1 oz) Cointreau *or* Curaçao
ice to mix

Rub the rims of 2 glasses with the lime wedge, and dip the wet edges into coarse salt. Rotate to coat the rims evenly. Combine the tequila, lime juice, orange liqueur and ice in a shaker. Shake and strain into the glasses.

RED WINE AND FRUIT
SANGRIA

Serves: 6-8

MEXICO, ARGENTINA

1 x 750 ml (26 oz) bottle red wine
½ cup lemon juice
½ cup lime juice *or* ½ cup orange juice
½ cup sugar
soda water, optional
ice cubes

Combine the lemon juice, lime or orange juice and sugar in a jug and stir to dissolve sugar. Add the wine and mix well. Chill and serve or pour the *sangria* over ice cubes in glasses. Soda may be added if desired — this is often done in Argentina but not in Mexico.

STRAWBERRY FIZZ
FRESA FIZZ ARGENTINA

Serves: 1

6 strawberries
1 tablespoon lemon juice
1 teaspoon sugar
champagne to fill glass

Mash the strawberries with the lemon juice and sugar. Place in a champagne glass and fill with chilled champagne.

Variation: PINEAPPLE FIZZ
ANNANA FIZZ

Substitute 2 tablespoons crushed pineapple with juice for the strawberries and lemon juice. Top with champagne.

These are special drinks served at the midnight *cena* (supper) on Christmas Eve or New Year's Eve and on other special occasions.

The following two recipes are based on the light Brazilian rum known as cachaça *or* aguadente. *The local white rums I have used here do not seem to resemble them in flavour. More acceptable results are obtained using the widely available Jamaican white rums in place of the sometimes unprocurable* cachaça.

RUM AND LEMON COCKTAIL.
BATIDA DE LIMAO BRAZIL

Serves: 2

60 ml (2 oz) light rum
⅛ cup lemon juice
3 teaspoons sugar

Mix all ingredients and pour over ice cubes in tall glasses.

RUM WITH LEMON WEDGES
CAIPHIRINHA BRAZIL

Serves: 2

60 ml (2 oz) light rum
2 lemons
3 teaspoons sugar

Pour the rum into 2 glasses. Wash the lemons and cut them into small wedges. Place half into each glass and add sugar to taste. Use the back of a spoon or a wooden pestle to crush and grind the lemon in the glass. The wedges are left in the drink which is slightly more bitter than the previous recipes. Add ice and serve.

COFFEE AND RUM COCKTAIL
BATIDA DE CAFE   *BRAZIL*

Serves: 2

60 ml (2 oz) light rum
½ cup cold, strong coffee
1 tablespoon condensed milk

Mix rum, coffee and condensed milk and stir to combine well. Pour over ice into glasses.

HOT, SPICED RUM
QUENTAO   *BRAZIL*

This drink is traditionally served on St John's Day (24 June) when many parties are held in Brazil. The hot drink is warming during these and other winter celebrations.

Serves: 3-4
Cooking time: 5 minutes

1½ cups light rum
½ cup water
1½ tablespoons sugar
1 lemon, sliced
2 cinnamon sticks
4 cloves

Combine all ingredients in an enamel saucepan and heat to boiling point. Strain and serve in small mugs or cups.

EGGNOG
ROMPOPE   *MEXICO*

Serves: 4-6
Cooking time: 20 minutes

4 cups milk
1 piece cinnamon stick
½ cup sugar
½ teaspoon nutmeg
1 teaspoon vanilla essence
4 egg yolks
1 tablespoon rum, optional

Place milk, cinnamon stick and sugar into a large saucepan and heat to boiling point. Remove from heat and let stand for 10 minutes. Remove cinnamon and stir in the nutmeg and vanilla. Beat the egg yolks until light and frothy, then beat them into the hot milk. Return to the stove and stir over low heat for 10 minutes or until the eggnog is smooth and thick. Remove from heat and add the rum. Serve hot topped with ground cinnamon, or chill and serve cold.

BRAZILIAN COFFEE

BRAZIL

Brazilian coffee is strong and sweet and is served in tiny cups. In Latin America coffee beans are not ground but are pulverised to a near powder for coffee. Pulverised coffee is available in many countries in vacuum-sealed jars labelled 'Turkish-style pulverised coffee'.

Serves: 4

1½ cups water
1½ tablespoons sugar, or to taste
4 tablespoons pulverised coffee

Place the water and sugar into a pan and heat to just below boiling point. Stir in the coffee, reheat gently but do not allow to boil. Stand for 1 minute, then pour through a coffee filter into a warmed pot or jug. Serve in small 100 ml (3 oz) coffee cups.

LATIN AMERICAN BREAKFAST COFFEE
CAFE COM LEITE OR *CAFE CON LECHE*

LATIN AMERICA

Serves: 4

1 quantity Brazilian coffee
3½ cups hot milk

Place the brewed coffee into 4 large breakfast cups and fill with steaming hot milk.

Index